United States Congress

Rules of the Senate of the United States

Consisting of special rules of the Senate

United States Congress

Rules of the Senate of the United States
Consisting of special rules of the Senate

ISBN/EAN: 9783337175603

Printed in Europe, USA, Canada, Australia, Japan

Cover: Foto ©Suzi / pixelio.de

More available books at **www.hansebooks.com**

RULES

OF THE

SENATE OF THE UNITED STATES,

CONSISTING OF

SPECIAL RULES OF THE SENATE,

THE

JOINT RULES OF THE TWO HOUSES,

AND SUCH

PROVISIONS OF THE CONSTITUTION

AS RELATE TO

THE ORGANIZATION, POWER, PRIVILEGES, PROCEEDINGS, AND DUTIES

OF THE

SENATE OF THE UNITED STATES.

PRINTED FOR THE USE OF THE SENATE OF THE UNITED STATES.

WASHINGTON:
GOVERNMENT PRINTING OFFICE.
1862.

SPECIAL RULES

FOR

CONDUCTING BUSINESS

IN THE

SENATE OF THE UNITED STATES.

COMMENCEMENT OF DAILY SESSIONS.

1.——The *President* having taken the *chair*, and a *quorum* being present, the *journal* of the preceding day shall be read, to the end that any *mistake* may be corrected that shall be made in the entries.

[16 April, 1789.

BUSINESS NOT TO BE INTERRUPTED.

2.——No member shall speak to another, or otherwise *interrupt the business* of the Senate, or read any newspaper, while the journals or public papers are *reading*, or when any member is *speaking* in any debate.

[16 April, 1789—14 Feb., 1828.

RULES IN SPEAKING OR DEBATE.

3.——Every member, when he *speaks*, shall address the Chair, standing in his place, and when he has finished shall sit down.

[16 April, 1789.

4.——No member shall *speak* more than *twice*, in any one debate, on the same day, without leave of the Senate.

[16 April, 1789.

5.——When *two members rise* at the same time, the President shall name the person to speak; but in all cases the member who shall first rise and address the Chair shall *speak first.*

[16 April, 1789—14 Feb., 1828.

CALLS TO ORDER AND APPEALS.

6.——If any member in speaking, or otherwise, transgress the *rules* of the Senate, the presiding officer shall, or any member may, *call to order*, and when a member shall be called to order by the President, or a senator, he shall sit down, and shall not proceed without leave of the Senate. And every *question of order* shall be decided by the President, without debate, subject to an *appeal* to the Senate; and the President may call for the sense of the Senate on any question of order.

[16 April, 1789—14 Feb., 1828—26 June, 1856.

EXCEPTIONABLE WORDS.

7.——If the member be called to order by a senator for words spoken, the *exceptional words* shall immediately be taken down in writing, that the President may be better able to judge of the matter.

[16 April, 1789.

ABSENT MEMBERS MAY BE SENT FOR.

8.——No member shall *absent* himself from the service of the Senate, without leave of the Senate first obtained. And in case a *less number than a quorum* of the Senate shall convene, they are hereby authorized to send the Sergeant-at-arms, or any other person or persons by them authorized, for any or all *absent members*, as the majority of such members present shall agree, at the expense of such absent members, respectively, unless such excuse for non-attendance shall be made as the Senate, when a *quorum* is convened, shall judge sufficient, and in that case the expense shall be paid out of the contingent fund.. And this rule shall apply as well to the first convention of the Senate, at the legal time of meeting, as to each day of the session, after the hour has arrived to which the Senate stood adjourned.

[16 April, 1789—25 June, 1798—14 Feb., 1828.

RULES FOR DEBATE.

9.——No motion shall be *debated* until the same shall be seconded.

[16 April, 1789.

RULE FOR MOTIONS, DEBATE, AND WITHDRAWAL.

10.——When *a motion* shall be made and seconded, it shall be reduced to writing, if desired by the President, or any member, delivered in at the table, and read, before the same shall be *debated;* and any motion may be *withdrawn* by the mover at any time before a decision, amendment, or ordering of the yeas and nays, except a motion to *reconsider*, which shall not be withdrawn without leave of the Senate.

[16 April, 1789—14 Feb., 1828—21 Jan., 1851.

PRECEDENCE OF MOTIONS WHEN QUESTION IS UNDER DEBATE.

11.——When a question is under *debate*, no motion shall be received but—

> to *adjourn*,
> to *lie on the table*,
> to *postpone indefinitely*,
> to *postpone to a day certain*,
> to *commit*, or
> to *amend*;

which several motions shall have precedence in the order they stand arranged; and the motion for *adjournment* shall always be in order, and be decided without debate.

[16 April, 1789—3 Jan., 1820—14 Feb., 1828.

DIVISION OF A QUESTION.

12.——If the *question* in debate contain several points, any member may have the same *divided;* but, on a motion to strike out and insert, it shall not be in order to move for a division of the question; but the rejection of a motion to *strike out* and *insert* one proposition shall not prevent a motion to strike out and insert a different proposition; nor prevent a subsequent motion simply to strike out; nor shall the rejection of a motion simply to strike out prevent a subsequent motion to strike out and insert.

[16 April, 1789—23 June, 1832.

FILLING BLANKS.

13.——In filling up *blanks*, the largest sum and longest time shall be first put.

[16 April, 1789—3 Jan., 1820—14 Feb., 1828.

OBJECTION TO READING A PAPER.

14.——When the *reading* of a paper is called for, and the same is *objected to* by any member, it shall be determined by a vote of the Senate, and without debate.

[3 Jan., 1820—14 Feb., 1828.

UNFINISHED BUSINESS—PRIOR SPECIAL ORDER.

15.——The *unfinished business* in which the Senate was engaged at the last preceding adjournment shall have the preference in the *special orders* of the day.

[3 Jan., 1820—14 Feb., 1828.

RULES FOR YEAS AND NAYS.

16.——When the *yeas* and *nays* shall be called for by *one-fifth* of the members present, each member called upon shall, unless for special reason he be excused by the Senate, declare openly, and without debate, his assent or dissent to the question. In taking the yeas and nays, and upon the call of the house, the names of the members shall be taken *alphabetically*.

[16 April, 1789.

17.——When the *yeas* and *nays* shall be taken upon any question, in pursuance of the above rule, no member shall be permitted, under any circumstances whatever, to *vote after the decision* is announced from the Chair.

[4 April, 1822—14 Feb., 1828.

RULE FOR CLOSING DOORS AND CLEARING GALLERY.

18.——On a motion made and seconded to *shut the doors* of the Senate, on the discussion of any business which may, in the opinion of a member, require *secrecy*, the President shall direct the *gallery* to be cleared; and during the discussion of such motion, the doors shall remain shut.

[20 Feb., 1794.

NO PERSON ADMITTED TO PRESENT PETITION, ETC.

19.——No motion shall be deemed in order *to admit any person* or persons whatsoever within the doors of the Senate chamber *to present* any *petition*, memorial, or address, or to hear any such read.

[27 April, 1798.

RULE FOR RECONSIDERATION.

20.——When *a question* has been once made and carried in the affirmative or negative, it shall be in order for any member of the majority to move for the *reconsideration* thereof; but no motion for the reconsideration of any vote shall be in order after a bill, resolution, message, report, amendment, or motion upon which the vote was taken, shall have gone out of the possession of the Senate, announcing their decision; nor shall any motion for *reconsideration* be in order, unless made on the same day on which the vote was taken, or within the two next days of actual session of the Senate thereafter.

[25 Feb., 1790—26 March, 1806

CASTING VOTE OF THE VICE-PRESIDENT.

21.——When the Senate are *equally divided*, the Secretary shall take the decision of the President.

[18 July, 1789.

QUESTION PUT BY PRESIDENT SENATE.

22.——All *questions* shall be *put* by the President of the Senate, either in the presence or absence of the President of the United States; and the senators shall signify their assent or dissent, by answering aye or no.

[21 Aug., 1789.

APPOINTMENT OF A MEMBER TO THE CHAIR.

23.——The Vice-President, or President of the Senate *pro tempore* shall have the right to name a member to perform the *duties of the Chair;* but such substitution shall not extend beyond an adjournment.

[3 Jan., 1820.

MORNING BUSINESS, PETITIONS, REPORTS, ETC.

24.——After the *journal* is read, the President shall first call for *petitions*, and then for *reports* from standing committees; and every petition, or memorial, or other paper, shall be *referred, of course,* without putting a question for that purpose, unless the reference is *objected* to by a member at the time such petition, memorial, or other paper, is presented. And before any petition or memorial, addressed to the Senate, shall be received and read at the table, whether the same shall be introduced by the President or a member, a *brief* statement of the *contents* of the petition or memorial shall verbally be made by the introducer.

[18 April, 1789—10 April, 1834.

NOTICE AND PRINTING OF BILLS, ETC.

25.——*One day's notice*, at least, shall be given of an intended motion for *leave* to bring in *a bill ;* and all bills reported by a committee shall, after the first reading, be *printed* for the use of the Senate; but no other paper or document shall be printed for the use of the Senate without special order.

[16 April, 1789—3 Jan., 1820—8 April, 1822—14 Feb., 1828.

ACTION ON BILLS, JOINT RESOLUTIONS, ETC., AND SUSPENSION OF JOINT RULES.

26.——Every *bill* shall receive *three readings* previous to its being passed, and the President shall give *notice at each*, whether it be the first, second, or third ; which reading shall be on three different days, unless the Senate unanimously direct otherwise. And all *resolutions* proposing amendments to the Constitution, or to which the approbation and signature of the President may be requisite, or which may *grant money out of the contingent or any other fund,* shall be treated, in all respects, in the introduction and form of proceedings on them, in the Senate, in a similar manner with *bills ;* and all other *resolutions* shall *lie on the table one day* for consideration, and *also reports of committees.* A motion to suspend, or to concur in a resolution of the House to suspend the 16*th* and 17*th joint rules,* or either of them, shall always be in *order*, be immediately considered, and be decided without debate.

[16 April, 1789—26 March, 1806—3 Jan., 1820—24 Feb., 1828—7 May, 1852.

Resolved, That the 26th rule of the Senate be repealed, so far as it may affect bills or joint resolutions of the Senate or House of Representatives proposing or providing for or relating to amendments to the Constitution of the United States.

[2 March, 1861.

COMMITMENT OF BILLS.

27.——No *bill* shall be committed or amended until it shall have been *twice read*, after which it may be *referred* to a committee.

[16 April, 1789.

IN COMMITTEE OF THE WHOLE.

28.——All *bills* on a second reading shall first be considered by the Senate in the same manner as if the Senate were *in committee of the whole*, before they shall be taken up and proceeded on by the Senate agreeably to the standing rules, unless otherwise ordered. And when the Senate shall consider a *treaty, bill*, or *resolution*, as *in committee* of the whole, the Vice-President, or President *pro tempore*, may call a member to fill the *chair* during the time the Senate shall remain in committee of the whole; and the *chairman* so called shall, during such time, have the *powers of a President pro tempore.*

[21 May, 1789—26 March, 1806--3 Jan., 1820.

FINAL QUESTIONS ON BILLS—REFERENCE TO COURT OF CLAIMS, ETC.

29.——The *final question* upon the *second reading* of every *bill, resolution*, constitutional amendment, or *motion*, originating in the Senate, and requiring *three readings* previous to being passed, shall be, ''Whether it shall be *engrossed* and read a third time?'' and no amendment shall be received for discussion at a *third reading* of any bill, resolution, amendment, or motion, unless by unanimous consent of the members present; but it shall at all times be *in order*, before the final passage of any such bill, resolution, constitutional amendment, or motion, *to move its commitment;* and should such commitment take place, and any amendment be reported by the committee, the said bill, resolution, constitutional amendment, or motion, shall be *again read a second time*, and considered as in committee of the whole, and then the aforesaid question shall be *again put.* Whenever a *private bill* is under consideration, it shall be in order to move, as a *substitute for* it, a resolution of the Senate referring the case to the *Court of Claims.*

[4 Feb., 1807—26 June, 1856.

AMENDMENTS TO APPROPRIATION BILLS.

30.——*No amendment* proposing additional *appropriations* shall be received to any *general appropriation bill*, unless it be made to carry out the provisions of some existing law, or some act or resolution, previously passed by the Senate, during that session, or moved by direction of a standing or select committee of the Senate, or in pursuance of an estimate from the head of some of the departments ; and *no amendments* shall be received whose object is to provide for a *private claim*, unless it be to carry out the provisions of an *existing law* or a *treaty* stipulation.

[19 Dec , 1850—7 May, 1852—13 Jan., 1854—3 May, 1854.

SPECIAL ORDERS.

31.——When the *hour* shall have arrived for the consideration of *a special order*, it shall be the duty of the Chair to take up such special order, and the Senate shall proceed to consider it, unless it be postponed by vote of the Senate.

[26 June, 1856.

PRECEDENCE IN SPECIAL ORDERS.

When *two or more subjects* shall have been *specially* assigned for consideration, they shall take *precedence* according to the order of time at which they were severally assigned, and such order shall at no time be lost or changed except by the direction of the Senate.

[26 June, 1856.

PRECEDENCE IN SPECIAL ORDERS AND OVER GENERAL ORDERS.

When *two or more subjects* shall have been assigned for the *same hour*, the subject *first assigned* for that hour shall take *precedence;* but *special orders* shall always have precedence of *general orders*, unless such special orders shall be postponed by direction of the Senate.

[26 June, 1856.

SPECIAL ORDERS NOT TO LOSE THEIR POSITION.

Special orders shall not lose their position on account of intervening adjournments; nor shall they lose their relative *position on the calendar*, except by vote of the Senate, until finally disposed of.

[26 June, 1856.

TWO-THIRDS REQUIRED TO MAKE A SPECIAL ORDER.

Provided, That no bill, joint resolution, or other subject, be made a special order for a particular day and hour without the concurrence of two-thirds of the senators present.

[13 January, 1862.

MAKING UP THE JOURNAL.

32.——The *titles* of *bills*, and such parts thereof only as shall be affected by proposed amendments, shall be *inserted on the journals*.

[12 March, 1792.

33.——The *proceedings* of the Senate, when not acting as in committee of the whole, shall be entered *on the journal* as concisely as possible, care being taken to detail a true and accurate account of the proceedings; but *every vote* of the Senate shall be entered on the journal, and a brief statement of the contents of each petition, memorial, or paper, presented to the Senate, shall also be inserted on the journal.

[19 May, 1789—12 March, 1792—14 Feb., 1828.

STANDING COMMITTEES.

34.——The following *standing committees* shall be appointed at the commencement of each session, with leave to report by bill or otherwise:

[5 March, 1857.

A Committee on *Foreign Relations*, to consist of seven members.

[10 Dec., 1816—5 March, 1857.

A Committee on *Finance*, to consist of seven members.
[10 Dec., 1816—5 March, 1857.

A Committee on *Commerce*, to consist of seven members.
[10 Dec., 1816—7 Dec., 1825—5 March, 1857.

A Committee on *Military Affairs* and the *Militia*, to consist of seven members.
[10 Dec., 1816—5 March, 1857.

A Committee on *Naval Affairs*, to consist of seven members.
[10 Dec., 1816—5 March, 1857.

A Committee on the *Judiciary*, to consist of seven members.
[10 Dec., 1816—5 March, 1857.

A Committee on *Post Offices* and *Post Roads*, to consist of seven members.
[10 Dec., 1816—5 March, 1857.

A Committee on *Public Lands*, to consist of seven members.
[10 Dec., 1816—5 March, 1857.

A Committee on *Private Land Claims*, to consist of five members.
[27 Dec., 1826—5 March, 1857.

A Committee on *Indian Affairs*, to consist of seven members.
[3 Jan., 1820—5 March, 1857.

A Committee on *Pensions*, to consist of seven members.
[10 Dec., 1816—5 March, 1857.

A Committee on *Revolutionary Claims*, to consist of five members.
[28 Dec., 1832—5 March, 1857.

A Committee on *Claims*, to consist of seven members.
[10 Dec., 1816—5 March, 1857—26 Jan., 1860.

A Committee on the *District of Columbia*, to consist of seven members.
[18 Dec., 1816—5 March, 1857.

A Committee on *Patents* and the *Patent Office,* to consist of five members.

[7 Sept., 1837—5 March, 1857.

A Committee on *Public Buildings* and *Grounds,* to consist of five members, who shall have power also to act jointly with the same committee of the House of Representatives.

[16 Dec., 1819—19 Dec., 1837—28 May, 1850—5 March, 1857.

A Committee on *Territories,* to consist of seven members.

[25 March, 1844—5 March, 1857.

A Committee to *Audit* and *Control* the *Contingent Expenses* of the Senate, to consist of three members, to whom shall be referred all resolutions directing the payment of money out of the contingent fund of the Senate, or creating a charge on the same.

[4 Nov., 1807—7 April, 1853—5 March, 1857.

PRINTING.

A Committee on *Printing,* to consist of three members, to whom shall be referred every question on the printing of documents, reports, or other matter transmitted by either of the executive departments, and all memorials, petitions, accompanying documents, together with all other matter, the printing of which shall be moved, *excepting* bills originating in Congress, resolutions offered by any senator, communications from the legislatures, or conventions lawfully called of the respective States, and motions to print by order of the standing committees of the Senate; motions to print *additional numbers* shall likewise be referred to said committee; and when the report shall be in favor of printing additional numbers, it shall be accompanied by *an estimate* of the probable cost; the said committee shall also supervise and direct the procuring of *maps and drawings* accompanying documents ordered to be printed.

[15 Dec., 1841—18 Dec., 1850—22 Jan., 1855—5 March, 1857.

A Committee on *Engrossed Bills*, to consist of three members, whose duty it shall be to examine all bills, amendments, resolutions, or motions, before they go out of the possession of the Senate; and shall deliver the same to the Secretary of the Senate, who shall enter upon the journal that the same have been correctly engrossed.

[3 Jan., 1820.

A Committee on *Enrolled Bills*, to consist of three members.

[6 Aug., 1789—5 March, 1857.

APPOINTMENT OF COMMITTEES.

35.——In the *appointment* of the *standing committees*, the Senate will proceed, by *ballot*, severally to appoint the *chairman* of each committee, and then, by one ballot, the other members necessary to complete the same; and *a majority* of the whole number of votes given shall be necessary to the choice of *a chairman* of a standing committee. All other committees shall be appointed by ballot; and *a plurality* of votes shall make a choice. When any *subject* or matter shall have been *referred* to a committee, any other subject or matter of a similar nature may, on motion, be referred to such committee.

[3 Jan., 1820—8 Dec., 1826—14 Feb., 1828.

REFERENCE TO STANDING OR SELECT COMMITTEES.

36.——When motions are made for *reference* of the same subject to a *select* committee, and to a *standing committee*, the question on reference to the standing committee shall be first put.

[14 Feb., 1828.

Rule 35—*Note.*—January 19, 1848. The Senate decided that in filling a vacancy on a committee, caused by the resignation of a chairman, by the President of the Senate, in accordance with an order of the Senate, it shall be only to fill up the number on the committee.

EXECUTIVE BUSINESS—PROCEEDINGS ON NOMINATIONS.

37.——When *nominations* shall be made in writing by the President of the United States to the Senate, a future day shall be assigned, unless the Senate unanimously direct otherwise, for taking them into consideration. *Nominations* neither approved nor rejected during the session at which they are made shall not be acted upon at any succeeding session without being again made by the President. When the *President of the United States* shall meet the Senate in the Senate chamber, the *President of the Senate* shall have a chair on the floor, be considered as the head of the Senate, and his chair shall be assigned to the President of the United States. When the Senate shall be convened by the President of the United States to any other place, the President of the Senate and senators shall attend at the place appointed. The Secretary of the Senate shall also attend to take the minutes of the Senate.

[21 Aug., 1789—18 Feb., 1843.

PROCEEDINGS ON TREATIES.

38.——Whenever *a treaty* shall be laid before the Senate for *ratification*, it shall be *read a first time* for information only; when no motion to reject, ratify, or modify the whole, or any part, shall be received. Its *second reading* shall be for consideration and on a subsequent day; when it shall be taken up as in committee of the whole, and every one shall be free to move a question on any particular article, in this form: "*Will the Senate advise and consent to the ratification of this article?*" or to propose *amendments* thereto, either by inserting or leaving out words; in which last case, the question shall be, "*Shall these words stand as part of the article?*" And in every of the said cases, the *concurrence* of *two-thirds* of the senators present shall be requisite to decide affirmatively. And when through the whole, the proceedings shall be stated to the House, *and questions shall be again severally put* thereon for confirmation, or new ones proposed, requiring, in like manner, a concurrence of *two-thirds*, for whatever is retained or inserted; the votes so confirmed shall, by the House, or a committee thereof, be reduced into the form of a *ratification*, with or without modifications, as may have been decided, and shall be proposed on a subsequent day, when every one shall again be free to move amendments, either by inserting or leaving out words; in which last case, the question shall be, "*Shall these words stand as part of the resolution?*" And in both cases the concurrence of *two-thirds* shall be requisite to carry the affirmative, as well as on the final question to advise and consent to the *ratification* in the form agreed to.

[6 Jan., 1801.

MATTERS CONFIDENTIAL AND SECRET.

39.—— All *confidential communications*, made by the President of the United States to the Senate, shall be by the members thereof *kept secret*, and *all treaties* which may be laid before the Senate shall also be *kept secret*, until the Senate shall, by their resolution, take off the *injunction of secrecy*.

[22 Dec., 1800—3 Jan., 1820.

SECRECY OF REMARKS ON NOMINATIONS.

40.——All information or *remarks* touching or concerning the *character* or qualifications of any person nominated by the President to office shall be *kept a secret*.

[3 Jan., 1820.

2

CLEARING OF THE SENATE

41.——When acting on *confidential* or *executive business*, the *Senate shall be cleared* of all persons except the Secretary, the principal or executive clerk, the Sergeant-at-arms and doorkeeper, and the assistant doorkeeper.

[3 Jan., 1820.

THREE SEPARATE JOURNALS TO BE KEPT.

42.——The *legislative proceedings*, the *executive proceedings*, and the *confidential legislative proceedings* of the Senate, shall be kept in separate and *distinct books*.

[19 May, 1789—15 April, 1828.

EXECUTIVE PROCEEDINGS FURNISHED TO THE PRESIDENT.

43.——The *President* of the United States shall, from time to time, be furnished with an authenticated transcript of the *executive records* of the Senate; and all *nominations* approved or definitely acted on by the Senate shall be *returned* by the Secretary, from day to day, as such proceedings may occur; but no further *extract* from the executive journal shall be furnished, except by special order; and *no paper*, except original treaties, transmitted to the Senate by the President of the United States, or any executive officer, *shall be returned* or delivered from the office of the Secretary without an order of the Senate for that purpose.

[27 Jan., 1792—27 March, 1818—5 Jan., 1829.

PROCEEDINGS ON AMENDMENTS TO THE CONSTITUTION.

44.——When an *amendment* to be proposed to the *Constitution* is under consideration, the concurrence of *two-thirds* of the members present shall not be requisite to decide any question for amendments, or extending to the merits, being short of the final question.

[26 March, 1806.

RECONSIDERATION.

45.——When any *question* may have been decided by the Senate, in which *two-thirds* of the members present are necessary to carry the affirmative, any member who votes on that side which prevailed in the question may be at liberty to move for a *reconsideration;* and a motion for reconsideration shall be decided by a *majority* of votes.

[3 Feb., 1801.

MESSAGES TO HOUSE OF REPRESENTATIVES.

46.——*Messages* shall be sent to the House of Representatives by the Secretary, who shall previously endorse the final determination of the Senate thereon.

[26 March, 1806.

MESSENGERS INTRODUCED.

47.——*Messengers* are *introduced* in any state of business, *except* while a question is putting, while the yeas and nays are calling, or while the ballots are counting.

[26 March, 1806.

PERSONS ADMITTED ON FLOOR.

48.——No person shall be admitted to the floor of the Senate, while in session, except as follows, viz: The officers of the Senate, members of the House of Representatives and their Clerk, the President of the United States and his private secretary, the heads of departments, foreign ministers, ex-Presidents and ex-Vice Presidents of the United States, ex-senators, senators elect, judges of the Supreme Court, and governors of States and Territories.

[17 March, 1853—23 January, 1854—24 January, 1854—6 March, 1856—11 January, 1859—
7 February, 1862.

REGULATION OF SENATE'S PART OF CAPITOL.

49.——The *presiding officer* of the Senate shall have the *regulation of such parts of the Capitol*, and of its passages, as are or may be set apart for the use of the Senate and its officers.

[22 Jan., 1824—14 Feb., 1828.

RESTRICTION ON PRESENTING REJECTED CLAIMS.

50.——Whenever *a claim* is presented to the Senate and referred to a committee, and the committee report that the claim *ought not to be allowed,* and the report be adopted by the Senate, it shall *not be in order* to move to take the papers from the *files* for the purpose of referring them at a subsequent session, *unless the claimant* shall present a memorial for that purpose, stating in what respect the committee have erred in their report, or that *new evidence* has been discovered since the report, and setting forth the new evidence, in the memorial: *Provided,* That this rule *shall not extend* to any case where an adverse report, not in writing, shall have been made prior to the 25th day of January, 1842.

[25 Jan., 1842—21 Dec., 1842.

PENALTIES FOR VIOLATING CONFIDENCE OF SENATE.

51.——Any officer or member of the Senate *convicted of disclosing* for publication any written or printed matter directed by the Senate to be held *in confidence,* shall be liable, if an officer, to *dismissal* from the service of the Senate, and in the case of a member, to suffer *expulsion* from the body.

JOINT RULES

OF

THE TWO HOUSES.

JOINT RULES AND ORDERS

OF

THE TWO HOUSES.

CONFERENCES.

1.——In every case of an amendment of a bill agreed to in one House, and dissented to in the other, if either House shall request *a conference*, and appoint a committee for that purpose, and the other House shall also appoint a committee to confer, such committees shall, at a convenient hour, to be agreed on by their chairmen, meet in the conference chamber, and state to each other, verbally or in writing, as either shall choose, the reasons of their respective Houses for and against the amendment, and confer freely thereon.

[15 April, 1789.

MESSAGE SENATE TO HOUSE OF REPRESENTATIVES.

2.——When *a message* shall be sent from the Senate to the House of Representatives, it shall be announced at the door of the House by the Doorkeeper, and shall be respectfully communicated to the Chair by the person by whom it may be sent.

MESSAGE HOUSE OF REPRESENTATIVES TO SENATE.

3.——The same ceremony shall be observed when a *message* shall be sent from the House of Representatives to the Senate.

BY WHOM MESSAGES MAY BE SENT.

4.——*Messages* shall be sent by such persons as a sense of propriety in each House may determine to be proper.

ENGROSSED BILLS.

5.——While *bills* are on their passage between the two Houses, they shall be *on paper*, and under the signature of the Secretary or Clerk of each House, respectively.

[6 August, 1789.

ENROLLED BILLS.

6.——After *a bill* shall have passed both Houses, it shall be duly *enrolled* on parchment by the Clerk of the House of Representatives, or the Secretary of the Senate, as the bill may have *originated* in the one or the other House, before it shall be presented to the President of the United States.

[6 August, 1789.

EXAMINATION OF ENROLLED BILLS.

7.——When *bills* are enrolled, they shall be *examined* by a joint *committee* of two from the Senate and two from the House of Representatives, appointed as a standing committee for that purpose, who shall carefully compare the *enrollment* with the *engrossed bills*, as passed in the two Houses, and, *correcting any errors* that may be discovered in the enrolled bills, make their report forthwith to their respective Houses.

[6 August, 1789—1 Feb., 1827.

SIGNING OF ENROLLED BILLS.

8.——After examination and report, each *bill* shall be *signed* in the respective Houses, first by the *Speaker* of the House of Representatives, then by the *President* of the Senate.

[6 August, 1789.

PRESENTATION OF ENROLLED BILLS TO THE PRESIDENT.

9.——After a bill shall have been thus signed in each House, it shall be *presented* by the said *committee* to the

President of the United States, for his *approbation*, (it being first endorsed on the ˜ back of the roll, certifying in which House the same *originated;* which endorsement shall be signed by the Secretary or Clerk, as the case may be, of the House in which the same did originate,) and shall be entered on the journal of each House.   The said *committee shall report* the day of *presentation* to the President; which time shall also be carefully entered on the journal of each House.

[6 August, 1789.

SAME PROCEEDINGS AS ABOVE ON ORDERS, RESOLUTIONS, AND VOTES, AS ON BILLS.

10.——*All orders, resolutions,* and *votes,* which are to be presented to the *President* of the United States for his approbation, shall also, in the same manner, be previously *enrolled, examined,* and *signed;* and shall be *presented* in the same manner, and by the same committee, as provided in the cases of bills.

[6 August, 1789.

JOINT ADDRESS TO THE PRESIDENT.

11.——When the Senate and House of Representatives shall judge it proper to make a *joint address* to the *President,* it shall be presented to him in his audience chamber by the President of the Senate, in the presence of the Speaker and both Houses.

[6 August, 1789.

NOTICE OF REJECTED BILL.

12.——When *a bill* or resolution which shall have passed in one House is *rejected* in the other, *notice* thereof shall be given to the House in which the same shall have passed.

[10 August, 1790.

REJECTED BILL NOT RENEWED WITHOUT TEN DAYS' NOTICE.

13.——When a *bill* or *resolution* which has been passed in one House shall be *rejected* in the other, it shall *not* be *brought in* during the same session, without a notice of ten days and leave of two-thirds of that House in which it shall be renewed.

[10 June, 1790.

PAPERS TO BE SENT WITH BILLS.

14.——*Each House* shall *transmit* to the other *all papers* on which any bill or resolution shall be founded.

[10 June, 1790.

ADHERENCE BY EACH HOUSE DESTROYS BILL.

15.——After *each House* shall have *adhered* to their disagreement, a *bill* or *resolution shall be lost.*

[10 June, 1790.

BILL NOT TO BE SENT TO OTHER HOUSE ON THREE LAST DAYS OF SESSION.

*16.——*No bill* that shall have passed one House *shall be sent* for concurrence to the other on either of the *last three days* of the session.

BILL NOT TO BE SENT TO THE PRESIDENT ON LAST DAY OF SESSION.

*17.——*No bill* or *resolution* that shall have passed the House of Representatives and the Senate *shall be presented* to the *President* of the United States, for his approbation, *on the last day* of the session.

PRINTING OF BILLS BY THE OTHER HOUSE.

18.——When *bills* which have passed one House are ordered to be *printed* in the other, a greater number of copies shall not be printed than may be necessary for the use of the House making the order.

[9 Feb., 1829.

---

* By the 26th Rule of Senate.—A motion to suspend or concur in resolution of H. R. to suspend the 16th or 17th Joint Rules, or either of them, shall always be in order, immediately considered, and decided without debate.

[7 May, 1852.

SALE OF INTOXICATING LIQUORS FORBIDDEN.

19.——No *intoxicating liquors* shall be offered for sale, or exhibited, within the Capitol, or on the public grounds adjacent thereto.

[18 Sep., 1837—H. R., 26 Feb., 1844—S., 30 May, 1844.

JOINT COMMITTEE ON THE LIBRARY.

20.——There shall be a *joint committee* on the *Library*, to consist of three members on the part of the Senate and three on the part of the House of Representative, to superintend and direct the expenditure of all moneys appropriated for the Library, and to perform such other duties as are or may be directed by law.

[S., 6 Dec., 1843—H. R., 7 Dec., 1843.

CONTINUANCE OF BUSINESS AT SUBSEQUENT SESSION.

21.——*After six days* from the commencement of a second or subsequent session of Congress, *all bills*, resolutions, or reports, which originated in either House, and at the close of the next preceding session remained undetermined in either House, *shall be resumed* and acted on in the same manner as if an adjournment had not taken place.

[14 August, 1848.

22.——When, during the present rebellion, any member of the Senate or House of Representatives shall rise, and, in his place, state that the President desires the immediate action of Congress upon any matter pertaining to the suppression of the present rebellion, the galleries of the House in which the statement is made shall be immediately cleared; and after such member shall state the action desired by the President, and the reasons for immediate action, such House shall determine, without debate, whether the proposed measure shall be considered. If decided in the affirmative, debate shall be confined to the subject matter, and be limited to five minutes by any member: *Provided*, That every member shall be allowed five minutes to explain or oppose any pertinent amendment: *And provided*, That this rule shall not affect the operation of the previous question in the House of Representatives.

During such session no communication shall be received or made to or from any person not a member then present, except through the President of the Senate or the Speaker of the House. If any member of the Senate or House of Representatives shall betray, publish, disclose, or reveal any debate, consultation, or procceding had in such secret session, he shall be expelled; and if committed by any officer of either body, or other person, such punishment shall be inflicted as the body to which he belongs may impose.

[30 January, 1862.

CONSTITUTION

OF THE

UNITED STATES OF AMERICA.

.

CONSTITUTION

UNITED STATES OF AMERICA.*

WE, the People of the United States, in order to form a more perfect Union, establish Justice, insure domestic Tranquillity, provide for the common defence, promote the general Welfare, and secure the Blessings of Liberty to ourselves and our Posterity, do ordain and establish this CONSTITUTION for the United States of America.

ARTICLE I.

SECTION 1. All legislative Powers herein granted shall be vested in a Congress of the United States, which shall consist of a Senate and House of Representatives.

SECTION 2. [1]The House of Representatives shall be composed of Members chosen every second Year by the people of the several States, and the Electors in each State shall have the Qualifications requisite for Electors of the most numerous Branch of the State Legislature.

[2]No Person shall be a Representative who shall not have attained to the Age of twenty-five Years, and been seven Years a Citizen of the United States, and who shall not, when elected, be an Inhabitant of that State in which he shall be chosen.

[3]Representatives and direct Taxes shall be apportioned among the several States, which may be included within this Union, according to their respective Numbers, which shall

* From Hickey's edition.

be determined by adding to the whole Number of free Per-
sons, including those bound to Service for a Term of Years,
and excluding Indians not taxed, three-fifths of all other
Persons. The actual Enumeration shall be made within
three Years after the first Meeting of the Congress of the
United States, and within every subsequent Term of ten
Years, in such manner as they shall by Law direct. The
Number of Representatives shall not exceed one for every
thirty thousand, but each State shall have at Least one
Representative ; and until such enumeration shall be made,
the State of New Hampshire shall be entitled to chuse three,
Massachusetts eight, Rhode-Island and Providence Planta-
tions one, Connecticut five, New-York six, New Jersey four,
Pennsylvania eight, Delaware one, Maryland six, Virginia
ten, North Carolina five, South Carolina five, and Georgia
three.

⁴When vacancies happen in the Representation from any
State, the Executive Authority thereof shall issue Writs of
Election to fill such Vacancies.

⁵The House of Representatives shall chuse their Speaker
and other Officers ; and shall have the sole Power of Impeachment.

SECTION 3. ¹The Senate of the United States shall be composed of two Senators from each State, chosen by the Legislature thereof, for six Years ; and each Senator shall have
one Vote.

²Immediately after they shall be assembled in Consequence of the first Election, they shall be divided as equally
as may be into three Classes. The Seats of the Senators of
the first Class shall be vacated at the Expiration of the
second year, of the second Class at the Expiration of the
fourth year, and of the third Class at the Expiration of the
sixth year, so that one-third may be chosen every second
Year ; and if Vacancies happen by Resignation, or other-

wise, during the recess of the Legislature of any State, the Executive thereof may make temporary Appointments until the next Meeting of the Legislature, which shall then fill such Vacancies.

³No Person shall be a Senator who shall not have attained to the Age of thirty Years, and been nine Years a Citizen of the United States, and who shall not, when elected, be an Inhabitant of that State for which he shall be chosen.

⁴The Vice President of the United States shall be President of the Senate, but shall have no Vote, unless they be equally divided.

⁵The Senate shall chuse their other Officers, and also a President pro tempore, in the Absence of the Vice President, or when he shall exercise the Office of President of the United States.

⁶The Senate shall have the sole Power to try all Impeachments. When sitting for that Purpose, they shall be on Oath or Affirmation. When the President of the United States is tried, the Chief Justice shall preside : And no Person shall be convicted without the Concurrence of two thirds of the Members present.

⁷Judgment in Cases of Impeachment shall not extend further than to removal from Office, and Disqualification to hold and enjoy any Office of honour, Trust or Profit under the United States : but the Party convicted shall nevertheless be liable and subject to Indictment, Trial, Judgment and Punishment, according to Law.

SECTION 4. ¹The Times, Places and Manner of holding Elections for Senators and Representatives, shall be prescribed in each State by the Legislature thereof ; but the Congress may at any time by Law make or alter such Regulations, except as to the places of chusing Senators.

²The Congress shall assemble at least once in every Year,

3

and such Meeting shall be on the first Monday in December, unless they shall by Law appoint a different day.

SECTION 5. [1] Each House shall be the Judge of the Elections, Returns and Qualifications of its own Members, and a Majority of each shall constitute a Quorum to do Business; but a smaller Number may adjourn from day to day, and may be authorized to compel the Attendance of absent Members, in such Manner, and under such Penalties as each House may provide.

[2] Each House may determine the Rules of its Proceedings, punish its Members for disorderly Behaviour, and, with the Concurrence of two thirds, expel a Member.

[3] Each House shall keep a Journal of its Proceedings, and from time to time publish the same, excepting such Parts as may in their Judgment require Secrecy: and the Yeas and Nays of the Members of either House on any question shall, at the Desire of one fifth of those Present, be entered on the Journal.

[4] Neither House, during the Session of Congress, shall, without the Consent of the other, adjourn for more than three days, nor to any other Place than that in which the two Houses shall be sitting.

SECTION 6. [1] The Senators and Representatives shall receive a Compensation for their Services, to be ascertained by Law, and paid out of the Treasury of the United States. They shall in all Cases, except Treason, Felony and Breach of the Peace, be privileged from Arrest during their Attendance at the Session of their respective Houses, and in going to and returning from the same; and for any Speech or Debate in either House, they shall not be questioned in any other Place.

[2] No Senator or Representative shall, during the Time for which he was elected, be appointed to any civil Office under the Authority of the United States, which shall have

been created, or the Emoluments whereof shall have been encreased during such time ; and no Person holding any Office under the United States, shall be a Member of either House during his Continuance in Office.

SECTION 7. [1]All Bills for raising Revenue shall originate in the House of Representatives ; but the Senate may propose or concur with Amendments as on other Bills.

[2]Every Bill which shall have passed the House of Representatives and the Senate, shall, before it become a Law, be presented to the President of the United States; If he approve he shall sign it, but if not he shall return it, with his Objections to that House in which it shall have originated, who shall enter the Objections at large on their Journal, and proceed to reconsider it. If after such Reconsideration two thirds of that House shall agree to pass the Bill, it shall be sent, together with the Objections, to the other House, by which it shall likewise be reconsidered, and if approved by two thirds of that House, it shall become a Law. But in all such Cases the Votes of both Houses shall be determined by yeas and Nays, and the Names of the Persons voting for and against the Bill shall be entered on the Journal of each House respectively. If any Bill shall not be returned by the President within ten Days (Sundays excepted) after it shall have been presented to him, the Same shall be a law, in like Manner as if he had signed it, unless the Congress by their Adjournment prevent its Return, in which Case it shall not be a Law.

[3]Every Order, Resolution, or Vote to which the Concurrence of the Senate and House of Representatives may be necessary (except on a question of Adjournment) shall be presented to the President of the United States; and before the Same shall take Effect, shall be approved by him, or being disapproved by him, shall be repassed by two-thirds of the Senate and House of Representatives, according to the Rules and Limitations prescribed in the Case of a Bill.

SECTION 8. The Congress shall have Power

¹To lay and collect Taxes, Duties, Imposts and Excises, to pay the Debts and provide for the common Defence and general Welfare of the United States; but all Duties, Imposts and Excises shall be uniform throughout the United States;

²To borrow Money on the credit of the United States;

³To regulate Commerce with foreign Nations, and among the several States, and with the Indian Tribes;

⁴To establish an uniform Rule of Naturalization, and uniform Laws on the subject of Bankruptcies throughout the United States;

⁵To coin Money, regulate the Value thereof, and of foreign Coin, and fix the Standard of Weights and Measures;

⁶To provide for the Punishment of counterfeiting the Securities and current Coin of the United States;

⁷To establish Post Offices and post Roads;

⁸To promote the progress of Science and useful Arts, by securing for limited Times to Authors and Inventors the exclusive Right to their respective Writings and Discoveries;

⁹To constitute Tribunals inferior to the Supreme Court;

¹⁰To define and punish Piracies and Felonies committed on the high Seas, and Offences against the Law of Nations;

¹¹To declare War, grant Letters of Marque and Reprisal, and make Rules concerning Captures on Land and Water;

¹²To raise and support Armies, but no Appropriation of Money to that Use shall be for a longer Term than two Years;

¹³To provide and maintain a Navy;

¹⁴To make Rules for the Government and Regulation of the land and naval Forces;

¹⁵To provide for calling forth the Militia to execute the Laws of the Union, suppress Insurrections and repel Invasions;

[16]To provide for organizing, arming, and disciplining the Militia, and for governing such Part of them as may be employed in the Service of the United States, reserving to the States respectively the Appointment of the Officers and the Authority of training the Militia according to the Discipline prescribed by Congress.

[17]To exercise exclusive Legislation in all Cases whatsoever, over such District (not exceeding ten Miles square) as may, by Cession of particular States, and the Acceptance of Congress, become the Seat of the Government of the United States, and to exercise like Authority over all places purchased by the Consent of the Legislature of the State in which the Same shall be, for the Erection of Forts, Magazines, Arsenals, Dock-Yards, and other needful Buildings ;—And

[18]To make all Laws which shall be necessary and proper for carrying into Execution the foregoing Powers, and all other Powers vested by this Constitution in the Government of the United States, or in any Department or Officer thereof.

SECTION 9. [1]The Migration or Importation of such Persons as any of the States now existing shall think proper to admit, shall not be prohibited by the Congress prior to the Year one thousand eight hundred and eight, but a Tax or Duty may be imposed on such Importation, not exceeding ten dollars for each Person.

[2]The Privilege of the Writ of Habeas Corpus shall not be suspended, unless when in Cases of Rebellion or Invasion the Public Safety may require it.

[3]No Bill of Attainder or ex post facto Law shall be passed.

No Capitation, or other direct, Tax shall be laid, unless in Proportion to the Census or Enumeration herein before directed to be taken.

[5]No Tax or Duty shall be laid on Articles exported from any State.

[6] No Preference shall be given by any Regulation of Commerce or Revenue to the Ports of one State over those of another : nor shall Vessels bound to, or from, one State, be obliged to enter, clear, or pay Duties in another.

[7] No Money shall be drawn from the Treasury, but in Consequence of Appropriations made by Law ; and a regular Statement and Account of the Receipts and Expenditures of all public Money shall be published from time to time.

[8] No Title of Nobility shall be granted by the United States : And no Person holding any Office of Profit or Trust under them, shall, without the Consent of the Congress, accept of any present, Emolument, Office, or Title, of any kind whatever, from any King, Prince, or foreign State.

SECTION 10. [1] No State shall enter into any Treaty, Alliance, or Confederation ; grant Letters of Marque and Reprisal ; coin Money ; emit Bills of Credit ; make any Thing but gold and silver Coin a Tender in Payment of Debts ; pass any Bill of Attainder, ex post facto Law, or Law impairing the Obligation of Contracts, or grant any Title of Nobility.

[2] No State shall, without the consent of the Congress, lay any Imposts or Duties on Imports or Exports, except what may be absolutely necessary for executing it's inspection Laws : and the net Produce of all Duties and Imposts, laid by any State on Imports or Exports, shall be for the Use of the Treasury of the United States ; and all such Laws shall be subject to the Revision and Controul of the Congress.

[3] No State shall, without the Consent of Congress, lay any Duty of Tonnage, keep Troops, or Ships of War in time of Peace, enter into any Agreement or Compact with another State, or with a foreign Power, or engage in War, unless actually invaded, or in such imminent Danger as will not admit of Delay.

, ARTICLE II.

SECTION 1. [1]The executive Power shall be vested in a President of the United States of America.   He shall hold his Office during the Term of four Years, and, together with the Vice President, chosen for the same Term, be elected, as follows :

[2]Each State shall appoint, in such Manner as the Legislature thereof may direct, a Number of Electors, equal to the whole Number of Senators and Representatives to which the State may be entitled in the Congress : but no Senator or Representative, or Person holding an Office of Trust or Profit under the United States, shall be appointed an Elector.

[[*] The Electors shall meet in their respective States, and vote by Ballot for two Persons, of whom one at least shall not be an Inhabitant of the same State with themselves.   And they shall make a List of all the Persons voted for, and of the Number of Votes for each ; which List they shall sign and certify, and transmit sealed to the Seat of the Government of the United States, directed to the President of the Senate.   The President of the Senate shall, in the Presence of the Senate and House of Representatives, open all the Certificates, and the Votes shall then be counted.   The Person having the greatest Number of Votes shall be the President, if such Number be a Majority of the whole Number of Electors appointed ; and if there be more than one who have such Majority, and have an equal Number of Votes, then the House of Representatives shall immediately chuse by Ballot one of them for President ; and if no Person have a Majority, then from the five highest on the List the said House shall in like Manner chuse the President.   But in chusing the President, the Votes shall be taken by States, the Representation from each State having one Vote ; A Quorum for this Purpose shall consist of a Member or Members from two thirds of the States, and a Majority of all the States shall be necessary to a Choice.   In every Case, after the Choice of the President, the Person having the greatest Number of Votes of the Electors shall be the Vice President.   But if there should remain two or more who have equal Votes, the Senate shall chuse from them by Ballot the Vice President.]

---

* This clause within brackets has been superceded and annulled by the 12th amendment, on page 49.

[3]The Congress may determine the Time of chusing the Electors, and the Day on which they shall give their Votes; which Day shall be the same throughout the United States.

[4]No Person except a natural born Citizen, or a Citizen of the United States, at the time of the Adoption of this Constitution, shall be eligible to the Office of President; neither shall any Person be eligible to that Office who shall not have attained to the Age of thirty-five Years, and been fourteen Years a Resident within the United States.

[5]In Case of the Removal of the President from Office, or of his Death, Resignation, or Inability to discharge the Powers and Duties of the said Office, the same shall devolve on the Vice President; and the Congress may by Law provide for the Case of Removal, Death, Resignation, or Inability, both of the President and Vice President, declaring what Officer shall then act as President, and such Officer shall act accordingly, until the Disability be removed, or a President shall be elected.

[6]The President shall, at stated Times, receive for his Services a Compensation, which shall neither be increased nor diminished during the Period for which he shall have been elected, and he shall not receive within that Period any other Emolument from the United States, or any of them.

[7]Before he enter on the Execution of his Office, he shall take the following Oath or Affirmation:

"I do solemnly swear (or affirm) that I will faithfully "execute the Office of President of the United States, and "will to the best of my Ability preserve, protect, and defend "the Constitution of the United States."

SECTION 2. [1]The President shall be Commander in Chief of the Army and Navy of the United States, and of the Militia of the several States, when called into the actual Service of the United States; he may require the Opinion, in writing, of the principle Officer in each of the executive Departments, upon any Subject relating to the Duties of their respective Offices, and he shall have Power to grant Reprieves and Pardons for Offences against the United States, except in Cases of Impeachment.

[2]He shall have Power, by and with the Advice and Consent of the Senate, to make Treaties, provided two-thirds of the Senators present concur; and he shall nominate, and by and with the Advice and Consent of the Senate shall appoint, Ambassadors, other public Ministers and Consuls, Judges of the Supreme Court, and all other Officers of the United States, whose Appointments are not herein otherwise provided for, and which shall be established by Law: but the Congress may by Law vest the Appointment of such inferior Officers as they think proper in the President alone, in the Courts of Law, or in the Heads of Departments.

[3]The President shall have Power to fill up all Vacancies that may happen during the Recess of the Senate, by granting Commissions which shall expire at the End of their next Session.

SECTION 3. He shall from time to time give to the Congress Information of the State of the Union, and recommend to their Consideration such Measures as he shall judge necessary and expedient; he may, on extraordinary Occasions, convene both Houses, or either of them, and in Case of Disagreement between them with Respect to the Time of Adjournment, he may adjourn them to such Time as he shall think proper; he shall receive Ambassadors and other public Ministers; he shall take Care that the Laws be faithfully executed, and shall Commission all the officers of the United States.

SECTION 4. The President, Vice-President, and all civil Officers of the United States, shall be removed from Office on Impeachment for, and Conviction of, Treason, Bribery, or other high Crimes and Misdemeanors.

ARTICLE III.

SECTION 1. The judicial Power of the United States, shall be vested in one Supreme Court, and in such inferior Courts as the Congress may from time to time ordain and establish. The Judges, both of the supreme and inferior Courts, shall hold their Offices during good Behavior, and shall, at stated Times, receive for their Services a Compensation, which shall not be diminished during their Continuance in Office.

SECTION 2. [1]The judicial Power shall extend to all Cases, in Law and Equity, arising under this Constitution, the Laws of the United States, and Treaties made, or which shall be made, under their Authority;—to all Cases affecting Ambassadors, other public Ministers, and Consuls;—to all Cases of admiralty and maritime Jurisdiction;—to Controversies to which the United States shall be a Party;—to Controversies between two or more States,—between a State and citizens of another State,—between Citizens of different States,—between Citizens of the same State claiming Lands under Grants of different States, and between a State, or the Citizens thereof, and foreign States, Citizens, or Subjects.

[2]In all Cases affecting Ambassadors, other public Ministers, and Consuls, and those in which a State shall be a Party, the Supreme Court shall have original Jurisdiction. In all the other Cases before mentioned, the Supreme Court shall have appellate Jurisdiction, both as to Law and Fact, with such Exceptions, and under such Regulations as the Congress shall make.

[3]The Trial of all Crimes, except in Cases of Impeachment, shall be by Jury; and such Trial shall be held in the State where the said Crimes shall have been committed; but when not committed within any State, the Trial shall be at such Place or Places as the Congress may by Law have directed.

SECTION 3. [1] Treason against the United States shall consist only in levying War against them, or in adhering to their Enemies, giving them Aid and Comfort. No Person shall be convicted of Treason unless on the Testimony of two Witnesses to the same overt Act, or on Confession in open Court.

[2] The Congress shall have Power to declare the Punishment of Treason, but no Attainder of Treason shall work Corruption of Blood, or Forfeiture except during the Life of the Person attainted.

ARTICLE IV.

SECTION 1. Full Faith and Credit shall be given in each State to the public Acts, Records, and judicial Proceedings of every other State. And the Congress may by general Laws prescribe the Manner in which such Acts, Records, and Proceedings shall be proved, and the Effect thereof.

SECTION 2. [1] The Citizens of each State shall be entitled to all Privileges and Immunities of Citizens in the several States.

[2] A Person charged in any State with Treason, Felony, or other Crime, who shall flee from Justice, and be found in another State, shall, on Demand of the executive Authority of the State from which he fled, be delivered up, to be removed to the State having Jurisdiction of the Crime.

[3] No Person held to Service or Labour in one State, under the Laws thereof, escaping into another, shall, in Consequence of any Law or Regulation therein, be discharged from such Service or Labour, but shall be delivered up on Claim of the Party to whom such Service or Labour may be due.

SECTION 3. [1] New States may be admitted by the Congress into this Union; but no new State shall be formed or erected within the Jurisdiction of any other State; nor any State be formed by the Junction of two or more States, or Parts of

States, without the Consent of the Legislatures of the States concerned as well as of the Congress.

²The Congress shall have Power to dispose of and make all needful Rules and Regulations respecting the Territory or other Property belonging to the United States; and nothing in this Constitution shall be so construed as to Prejudice any Claims of the United States, or of any particular State.

SECTION 4. The United States shall guarantee to every State in this Union a Republican Form of Government, and shall protect each of them against Invasion, and on Application of the Legislature, or of the Executive (when the Legislature cannot be convened) against domestic Violence.

ARTICLE V.

The Congress, whenever two thirds of both Houses shall deem it necessary, shall propose Amendments to this Constitution, or, on the Application of the Legislatures of two thirds of the several States, shall call a Convention for proposing Amendments, which, in either Case, shall be valid to all Intents and Purposes, as Part of this Constitution, when ratified by the Legislatures of three fourths of the several States, or by Conventions in three fourths thereof, as the one or the other Mode of Ratification may be proposed by the Congress; Provided that no Amendment which may be made prior to the Year one thousand eight hundred and eight shall in any Manner affect the first and fourth Clauses in the Ninth Section of the first Article; and that no State, without its Consent, shall be deprived of its equal Suffrage in the Senate.

ARTICLE VI.

¹All Debts contracted and Engagements entered into, before the Adoption of this Constitution, shall be as valid against

the United States under this Constitution, as under the Confederation.

[2]This Constitution, and the Laws of the United States which shall be made in pursuance thereof; and all Treaties made, or which shall be made, under the authority of the United States, shall be the supreme Law of the Land ; and the Judges in every State shall be bound thereby, any Thing in the Constitution or Laws of any State to the Contrary notwithstanding.

[3]The Senators and Representatives before mentioned, and the Members of the several State Legislatures, and all executive and judicial Officers, both of the United States and of the several States, shall be bound by Oath or Affirmation, to support this Constitution ; but no religious Test shall ever be required as a Qualification to any Office or public Trust under the United States.

ARTICLE VII.

The Ratification of the Conventions of nine States, shall be sufficient for the Establishment of this Constitution between the States so ratifying the Same.

Done in Convention by the Unanimous Consent of the States present the Seventeenth Day of September in the Year of our Lord one thousand seven hundred and Eighty seven and of the Independance of the United States of America the Twelfth. **In Witness** whereof We have hereunto subscribed our Names,

GEO WASHINGTON—

Presidt and deputy from Virginia

NEW HAMPSHIRE.

John Langdon,
Nicholas Gilman.

MASSACHUSETTS.

Nathaniel Gorham,
Rufus King.

CONNECTICUT.

Wm. Samuel Johnson,
Roger Sherman.

NEW YORK.

Alexander Hamilton.

NEW JERSEY.

Wil. Livingston,
David Brearley,
Wm. Paterson,
Jona. Dayton.

PENNSYLVANIA.

B. Franklin,
Thomas Mifflin,
Robert Morris,
Geo. Clymer,
Tho. Fitzsimons,
Jared Ingersoll,
James Wilson,
Gouv. Morris.

Attest:

DELAWARE.

Geo. Reed,
Gunning Bedford, Jun'r,
John Dickinson,
Richard Bassett,
Jaco. Broom.

MARYLAND.

James M'Henry,
Dan. of St. Thos. Jenifer,
Danl. Carroll.

VIRGINIA.

John Blair,
James Madison, Jr.

NORTH CAROLINA.

Wm. Blount,
Rich'd Dobbs Spaight,
Hu. Williamson.

SOUTH CAROLINA.

J. Rutledge,
Charles Cotesworth Pinckney,
Charles Pinckney,
Pierce Butler.

GEORGIA.

William Few
Abr. Baldwin.

WILLIAM JACKSON, *Secretary*.

The Constitution was adopted on the 17th September, 1787, by the convention appointed in pursuance of the resolution of the Congress of the Confederation, of the 21st February, 1787, and was ratified by the Conventions of the several States, as follows, viz :

By Convention of Delaware,	on the 7th December, 1787.
" " Pennsylvania,	" 12th December, 1787.
" " New Jersey,	" 18th December, 1787.
" " Georgia,	" 2d January, 1788.
" " Connecticut,	" 9th January, 1788.
" " Massachusetts,	" 6th February, 1788
" " Maryland,	" 28th April, 1788.
" " South Carolina,	" 23d May, 1788.
" " New Hampshire,	" 21st June, 1788.
" " Virginia,	" 26th June, 1788.
" " New York,	" 26th July, 1788.
" " North Carolina,	" 21st November, 1789.
" " Rhode Island,	" 29th May, 1790

ARTICLES

IN ADDITION TO, AND AMENDMENT OF,

THE CONSTITUTION

OF THE

UNITED STATES OF AMERICA,

Proposed by Congress, and ratified by the Legislatures of the several States, pursuant to the fifth article of the original Constitution.

(ARTICLE I.)

Congress shall make no law respecting an establishment of religion, or prohibiting the free exercise thereof; or abridging the freedom of speech, or of the press; or the right of the people peaceably to assemble, and to petition the Government for a redress of grievances.

(ARTICLE II.)

A well regulated militia, being necessary to the security of a free State, the right of the people to keep and bear Arms shall not be infringed.

(ARTICLE III.)

No soldier shall, in time of peace be quartered in any house, without the consent of the Owner, nor in time of war, but in a manner to be prescribed by law.

(ARTICLE IV.)

The right of the people to be secure in their persons, houses, papers, and effects, against unreasonable searches

4

and seizures, shall not be violated, and no Warrants shall issue, but upon probable cause, supported by Oath or affirmation, and particularly describing the place to be searched, and the persons or things to be seized.

(ARTICLE V.)

No person shall be held to answer for a capital, or otherwise infamous crime, unless on a presentment or indictment of a Grand Jury, except in cases arising in the land or naval forces, or in the Militia, when in actual service in time of War or public danger; nor shall any person be subject for the same offence to be twice put in jeopardy of life or limb; nor shall be compelled in any Criminal Case to be a witness against himself, nor be deprived of life, liberty, or property, without due process of law; nor shall private property be taken for public use, without just compensation.

(ARTICLE VI.)

In all criminal prosecutions, the accused shall enjoy the right to a speedy and public trial, by an impartial jury of the State and district wherein the crime shall have been committed, which district shall have been previously ascertained by law, and to be informed of the nature and cause of the accusation ; to be confronted with the witnesses against him ; to have Compulsory process for obtaining Witnesses in his favour, and to have the Assistance of Counsel for his defence.

(ARTICLE VII.)

In Suits at common law, where the value in controversy shall exceed twenty dollars, the right of trial by jury shall be preserved, and no fact tried by a jury shall be otherwise re-examined in any Court of the United States, than according to the rules of the common law.

(ARTICLE VIII.)

Excessive bail shall not be required, nor excessive fines imposed, nor cruel and unusual punishments inflicted.

(ARTICLE IX.)

The enumeration in the Constitution, of certain rights, shall not be construed to deny or disparage others retained by the people.

(ARTICLE X.)

The powers not delegated to the United States by the Constitution, nor prohibited by it to the States, are reserved to the States respectively, or to the people.

(ARTICLE XI.)

The Judicial power of the United States shall not be construed to extend to any suit in law or equity, commenced or prosecuted against one of the United States by Citizens of another State, or by Citizens or Subjects of any Foreign State.

(ARTICLE XII.)

The Electors shall meet in their respective States, and vote by ballot for President and Vice-President, one of whom, at least, shall not be an inhabitant of the same State with themselves; they shall name in their ballots the person voted for as President, and in distinct ballots the person voted for as Vice-President, and they shall make distinct lists of all persons voted for as President, and of all persons voted for as Vice-President, and of the number of votes for each, which lists they shall sign and certify, and transmit sealed to the seat of the government of the United States, directed to the President of the Senate;—The President of the Senate shall, in presence of the Senate and House of Representatives, open all the certificates and the votes shall then be counted;—The person having the greatest number of votes for President, shall be the President, if such number be a majority of the whole number of Electors appointed; and if no person have such majority, then from the persons having the highest numbers not exceeding three on the list of those voted for as President, the House of Representatives shall choose immediately, by ballot, the President.   But in choosing the President, the votes shall be taken by States, the represen-. tation from each State having one vote; a quorum for this purpose shall consist of a member or members from two-thirds of the States, and a majority of all the States shall be necessary to a choice.   And if the House of Representatives shall not choose a President whenever the right of choice shall devolve upon them, before the fourth day of March next following, then the Vice-President shall act as President, as in the case of the death or other constitutional disability of the President.   The person having the greatest number of votes as Vice-President, shall be the Vice-President, if such number be a majority of the whole number of Electors appointed, and if no person have a majority, then from the two highest numbers on the list, the Senate shall choose the Vice-President; a quorum for the purpose shall consist of two-thirds of the whole number of Senators, and a majority of the whole number shall be necessary to a choice.   But no person constitutionally ineligible to the office of President shall be eligible to that of Vice-President of the United States.

NOTE.—The ten first of the preceding amendments were proposed at the first session of the first Congress of the United States, 25 September, 1789, and were finally ratified by the constitutional number of States, on the 15th day of December, 1791.   The eleventh amendment was proposed at the first session of the third Congress, 5 March, 1784, and was declared in a message from the President of the United States to both houses of Congress, dated 8th January, 1798, to have been adopted by the constitutional number of States.   The twelfth amendment was proposed at the first session of the eighth Congress, 12 December, 1803, and was adopted by the constitutional number of States in 1804, according to a public notice thereof by the Secretary of State, dated 25th September, of the same year.

ANALYTICAL INDEX

OF THE

RULES OF THE SENATE.

PREPARED IN THE OFFICE OF THE SECRETARY OF THE SENATE.

PART I.

OF THE SPECIAL RULES OF THE SENATE.

PART II.

OF THE JOINT RULES OF THE TWO HOUSES.

PART III.

OF THE PROVISIONS OF THE CONSTITUTION AFFECTING THE ORGANIZATION, POWER, RULES, DUTIES, AND PROCEEDINGS OF THE SENATE.

INDEX OF PART FIRST.

SPECIAL RULES OF THE SENATE:

2

INDEX TO SPECIAL RULES OF SENATE.

No.

ADJOURNMENTS. Special orders not to lose their position on the calendar on account of intervening ... 31

ADMIT any person in Senate to present a petition, &c., &c. No motion in order to ... 19

ADMITTED on the floor of the Senate. Description of persons (and none others) who shall be ... 48

ALPHABETICALLY. In taking the yeas and nays, or on a call of the House, the names of the members taken ... 16

Amendments.

AMEND, &c., &c. When a question is under debate no motion shall be received but to ... 11

AMENDED until twice read, &c. No bill shall be ... 27

AMENDMENT. Any motion may be withdrawn before ... 10

AMENDMENTS containing several points may be divided, but a motion to strike out and insert shall not be divided. The rejection of a motion to strike out and insert one proposition, shall not prevent a motion to strike out and insert a different proposition, nor a motion simply to strike out, nor another motion to strike out and insert ... 12

AMENDMENTS to the Constitution same as on bills, &c. The proceedings on. 26

AMENDMENT. No amendment shall be received for discussion at a third reading of any bill, &c., unless by unanimous consent, but such bill, &c., may be referred to a committee, and should an amendment be reported, the bill, &c., shall again be read a second time, &c., (see Rule) ... 29

AMENDMENT shall be, "Whether it shall be engrossed and read a third time?" The final question on the second reading of any constitutional ... 29

AMENDMENT proposing additional appropriations shall not be received to any general appropriation bill, unless to carry out an existing law, or act, or resolution of the Senate previously passed, during that session, or moved by a standing or select committee, or in pursuance of an estimate from the head of some of the departments; and no amendment shall be received to provide for a private claim, unless it be to carry out an existing law or treaty stipulation ... 30

AMENDMENTS shall be inserted on the journals. The titles of bills and parts affected by ... 32

AMENDMENTS to treaties. Forms of questions and proceedings on ... 38

AMENDMENT to be proposed to the Constitution is under consideration, the concurrence of two-thirds of the members present shall not be requisite to decide any question for amendments, or extending to the merits, being short of the final question. When an ... 44

Rules of the Senate in relation to Bills.

4   INDEX TO SPECIAL RULES OF SENATE.

Rules relating to Committees.

Rules relating to Debate.

Rules relating to Executive Business.

Rules relating to the Journal.

Rules relating to members of the Senate.

Rules relating to Motions.

Rules relating to Order.

Orders of the Day.

Rules relating to Questions before the Senate.

Relating to Resolutions.

Rules relating to the Powers, Privileges, and Proceedings of the Senate.

34   INDEX TO SPECIAL RULES OF SENATE.

No.

34   INDEX TO SPECIAL RULES OF SENATE.

No.

SENATE for that purpose. No paper, except original treaties, transmitted to the Senate by the President of the United States, or any executive officer, shall be returned or delivered from the office of the Secretary without an order of the 43

SENATE, &c. The President of the United States shall, from time to time, be furnished with an authenticated transcript of the executive records of the ... 43

SENATE thereon. Messages shall be sent to the House of Representatives by the Secretary, who shall previously endorse the final determination of the 46

SENATE. Description of persons (and none others) who shall be admitted on the floor of the 48

SENATE shall have the regulation of such parts of the Capitol, and of its passages, as are or may be set apart for the use of the Senate and its officers. The presiding officer of the ... 49

SENATE. Restriction on presenting rejected claims to the (see *Rule*) 50

SENATE. Penalty of an officer or member for violating the confidence of the ... 51

SENATORS of the United States.—(See *Members*.)

SENSE of the Senate on any question of order. The President may call for the ... 6

SERGEANT-AT-ARMS, or any other authorized person, may be sent for absent members. The ... 8

SERGEANT-AT-ARMS and doorkeeper and assistant doorkeeper admitted in secret session. The ... 41

SESSION. Organization and commencement of business of each day's 1

SESSION, should less than a quorum appear, absent members may be sent for, &c. At the commencement or during any ... 8

SESSION of the Senate, if the matter is in possession of the Senate. A motion for reconsideration may be made within two next days of actual 20

SHUT the doors, the gallery shall be cleared. On a motion made and seconded to ... 18

Rules relating to Speaking and Debate in the Senate.

SPEAK shall address the Chair, stand at his place, and sit down when finished. Every member rising to ... 3

SPEAK more than twice in one debate on same day without leave of the Senate. No member shall ... 4

SPEAK first; but the member rising and addressing the Chair first shall speak first. When two members rise, the President shall name the member to ... 5

SPEAKING to another member so as to interrupt business prohibited 2

Rules relating to the Standing Committees of the Senate.

Standing committees of the Senate shall be appointed at the commencement
of each session, with leave to report by bill or otherwise, viz :

Rules relating to Proceedings on Treaties.

Rules relating to Votes in the Senate.

Rules relating to Yeas and Nays.

INDEX OF PART SECOND.

JOINT RULES OF THE TWO HOUSES OF CONGRESS.

42 INDEX TO JOINT RULES.

Rules relating to the President of the United States.

7

INDEX OF PART THIRD.

PROVISIONS IN THE CONSTITUTION AFFECTING THE ORGANIZATION, POWER, RULES, DUTIES, AND PROCEEDINGS OF THE SENATE.

AMENDMENTS. All bills for raising revenue shall originate in the House of Representatives, but the Senate may propose or concur with amendments, as on other bills.

Const , art. 1, sec. 7, cl. 1.

AMENDMENTS to the Constitution   Proceedings on.

Const., art. 5, sec. 1, cl. 1.

APPOINTED. No senator or representative shall, during the time for which he was elected, be appointed to any civil office under the authority of the United States which shall have been created, or the emoluments of which shall have been increased during such time.

Const., art. 1, sec. 6, cl. 2.

APPOINTED. No senator or representative, or person holding an office of trust or profit under the United States, shall be appointed an elector.

Const., art. 2, sec. 1, cl. 2.

APPOINTMENTS. The executives of States may make temporary appointments of senators in the recess of the legislatures thereof, to fill vacancies.

Const., art. 1, sec. 3, cl. 2.

APPOINTMENTS made by the President, by and with the advice and consent of the Senate.

Const., art. 2, sec. 2, cl. 2.

APPOINTMENTS during the recess of the Senate to expire at the end of their next session.   .

Const., art. 2, sec. 2, cl. 3.

APPROVED. Every bill, resolution, or vote, to which the concurrence of the Senate and House of Representatives may be necessary, (except on a question of adjournment,) shall be presented to the President of the United States, to be approved or disapproved by him.

Const., art. 1, sec. 7, cl. 2, 3.

APPROVED. Any bill, &c., returned by the President with objection, may become a law if approved by two-thirds of both houses of Congress.

Const., art. 1, sec. 7, cl. 2.

ARREST. Senators and representatives shall, in all cases, except treason, felony, and breach of the peace, be privileged from arrest during their attendance at the sessions of their respective houses, and in going to and returning from the same.

Const., art. 1, sec. 6, cl. 1.

ASSEMBLE. Congress shall assemble at least once in every year, on the first Monday in December, unless they shall by law appoint a different day.

Const., art. 1, sec. 4, cl. 2.

ATTENDANCE Less than a quorum of either house may compel the attendance of absent members.

Const., art. 1, sec. 5, cl. 1.

ATTENDANCE. Members of Congress privileged from arrest during their attendance at sessions, &c.

Const., art. 1, sec 6, cl. 1.

50 PROVISIONS IN THE CONSTITUTION

Bills. All bills for raising revenue shall originate in the House of Representatives, but the Senate may propose or concur with amendments, as on other bills, &c.

Const., art. 1, sec. 7, cl. 1.

BILL. Every bill which shall have passed the House of Representatives and Senate shall, before it become a law, be presented to the President of the United States; if he approve, he shall sign it; but if not, he shall return it, with his objections, to that house in which it shall have originated, who shall enter the objections at large on their journal, and proceed to reconsider it. If, after such reconsideration, two-thirds of that house shall agree to pass the bill, it shall be sent, together with the objections, to the other house, by which it shall likewise be reconsidered, and if approved by two-thirds of that house it shall become a law. But in all cases the votes of both houses shall be determined by yeas and nays, and the names of the persons voting for and against the bill shall be entered on the journal of each house, respectively.

Const., art. 1, sec. 7, cl. 2.

BILL. If any bill shall not be returned by the President within ten days (Sundays excepted) after it shall have been presented to him, the same shall be a law, in like manner as if he had signed it, unless the Congress, by their adjournment, prevent its return, in which case it shall not be a law.

Const., art. 1, sec. 7, cl. 2.

BILL. Every order, resolution, or vote, to which the concurrence of the Senate and House of Representatives may be necessary, (except on a question of adjournment,) shall be presented to the President of the United States; and before the same shall take effect shall be approved by him, or, being disapproved by him, shall be repassed by two-thirds of the Senate and House of Representatives, according to the rules and limitations prescribed in the case of a bill.

Const., art. 1, sec. 7, cl. 3.

BREACH of the peace. For a breach of the peace, a senator or representative may be arrested.

Const., art. 1, sec. 6, cl. 1.

BUSINESS. A majority of each house shall constitute a quorum to do business.

Const., art. 1, sec. 5, cl. 1.

Chief Justice shall preside when the President of the United States is tried on an impeachment by the Senate.

Const., art. 1, sec. 3, cl. 6.

CITIZEN of the United States. No person shall be a senator in Congress who has not been nine years a citizen of the United States.

Const., art. 1, sec. 3, cl. 3.

CLASSES. The senators shall be divided as equally as may be into three classes.

Const., art. 1, sec. 3, cl. 2.

COMPEL the attendance of absent members. A smaller number than a quorum of each house may compel the attendance of absent members, in such manner and under such penalties as each house may provide.

Const., art. 1, sec. 5, cl. 1.

COMPENSATION. The senators and representatives shall receive a compensation for their services, to be ascertained by law, and paid out of the treasury of the United States.

Const., art. 1, sec. 6, cl. 1.

CONCUR. The Senate may propose and concur in amendments to revenue bills, &c.

Const., art. 1, sec. 7, cl. 1.

CONCURRENCE. No person shall be convicted on an impeachment without the concurrence of two-thirds of the senators present.

Const., art. 1, sec. 3, cl. 6.

CONCURRENCE. Every order, resolution, or vote, to which the concurrence of the two houses may be necessary, shall be presented to the President, except on a question of adjournment, &c.

Const., art. 1, sec. 7, cl. 3.

CONSENT of either house. Neither house, during the session of Congress, shall, without the consent of the other, adjourn for more than three days, nor to any other place than that in which the houses shall be sitting.

Const., art. 1, sec. 5, cl. 4.

CONSENT. No State, without its consent, shall be deprived of its equal suffrage in the Senate.

Const., art. 5.

CONSTITUTION. The Congress, whenever two-thirds of both houses shall deem it necessary, shall propose amendments to this Constitution, &c., &c.

Const., art. 5.

CONSTITUTION. The senators, &c , shall be bound by oath or affirmation to support this Constitution.—(See *Oath*.)

Const., art. 6, ——, cl. 3.

CONVENE Congress. The President may, on extraordinary occasions, convene both houses, or either of them.

Const., art. 2, sec. 3, cl. 1.

CONVICTED. No person shall be convicted on an impeachment without the concurrence of two-thirds of the senators present.

Const., art. 1, sec. 3, cl. 6.

Debate. Senators and representatives, for any speech or debate in either house, shall not be questioned in any other place.

Const., art. 1, sec. 6, cl. 1.

DISORDERLY behavior. Each house may punish its members for disorderly behavior.

Const., art. 1, sec. 5, cl. 2.

DIVIDED. The Vice-President shall have no vote unless the Senate be equally divided.
Const., art. 1, sec. 3, cl. 4.

Elected. Two senators from each State shall be chosen or elected by the legislature thereof for six years.
Const., art. 1, sec. 3, cl. 1.

ELECT. The Senate shall elect or choose their other officers, and also a President *pro tempore,* in the absence of the Vice-President, or when he shall exercise the office of President of the United States.
Const., art. 1, sec. 3, cl. 5.

ELECTIONS. The times, places, and manner of holding elections for senators and representatives shall be prescribed in each State by the legislature thereof; but the Congress may, at any time, by law make or alter such regulations, except as to the places of choosing senators.
Const., art. 1, sec. 4, cl. 1.

ELECTIONS. Each house shall be the judge of the elections, returns, and qualifications of its own members.
Const., art. 1, sec. 5, cl. 1.

ELECTOR. No senator, &c., shall be appointed an elector of President or Vice-President of the United States, &c.
Const., art. 2, sec. 1, cl. 2.

ELIGIBILITY of a senator in Congress. No person shall be a senator who shall not have attained to the age of thirty years, and been nine years a citizen of the United States, and who shall not, when elected, be an inhabitant of that State for which he shall be chosen.
Const., art. 1, sec. 3, cl. 3.

EQUAL suffrage. No State, without its consent, shall be deprived of its equal suffrage in the Senate.
Const., art. 5.

EXPEL a member. Either house of Congress may, with the concurrence of two-thirds, expel a member.
Const., art. 1, sec. 5, cl. 2.

Happen. When vacancies happen by resignation or otherwise (in the office of senator) during the recess of the legislature of any State, the executive thereof may make temporary appointments, &c.
Const., art. 1, sec. 3, cl. 2.

HAPPEN. The President shall have power to fill up vacancies that may happen during the recess of the Senate, &c.
Const., art. 2, sec. 2, cl. 3.

Impeachments. The House of Representatives shall have the sole power of impeachment.
Const., art. 1, sec. 2, cl. 5.

IMPEACHMENTS. The Senate of the United States shall have the sole power to try all impeachments.
Const., art. 1, sec. 3, cl. 6.

IMPEACHMENT.   When sitting to try an impeachment, the Senate shall be on oath or affirmation.   When the President is tried the Chief Justice shall preside.   No person shall be convicted without the concurrence of two-thirds of the members present.   Judgment in cases of impeachment shall not extend further than removal from office, and disqualification to hold and enjoy any office of honor, trust, or profit, under the United States. But the party convicted shall, nevertheless, be liable and subject to indictment, trial, judgment, and punishment, according to law.

Const., art. 1, sec. 3, cl. 6.

INHABITANT.   A senator in Congress shall be an inhabitant of the State in which he shall be chosen.

Const., art. 1, sec. 3, cl. 3.

Journal.   Each house of Congress shall keep a journal of its proceedings, and from time to time publish the same, excepting such parts as may, in their judgment, require secrecy ; and the yeas and nays of the members of either house, on any question, shall, at the desire of one-fifth of those present, be entered on the journal.

Const., art. 1, sec. 5, cl. 3.

JOURNAL.   When the President shall return a bill, with his objections, to the house in which it originated, those objections shall be entered at large on their journal, and the votes, by yeas and nays, on the reconsideration of such bill, shall be entered on the journal of each house respectively.—(See *Bill.*)

Const., art. 1, sec. 7, cl. 2.

Legislative power.   All legislative powers herein granted shall be vested in a Congress of the United States, which shall consist of a Senate and House of Representatives.

Const., art. 1, sec. 1, cl. 1.

LEGISLATURE of each State shall choose two Senators for six years.   The.

Const., art. 1, sec. 3, cl. 1.

LEGISLATURE.   If vacancies happen by resignation or otherwise in the seats of senators during the recess of the legislature of any State, the executive thereof may make temporary appointments to fill such vacancies until the next meeting of the legislature, which shall then fill such vacancies.

Const., art. 1, sec. 3, cl. 2.

LEGISLATURE.   The times, places, and manner of holding elections for senators and representatives shall be prescribed in each State by the legislature thereof ; but the Congress may, at any time, by law make or alter such regulations, except as to the places of choosing senators.

Const., art. 1, sec. 4, cl. 1.

Majority of each house of Congress shall constitute a quorum to do business. A.

Const., art. 1, sec. 5, cl. 1.

MAJORITY of the whole number of senators shall be necessary to a choice of Vice-President when the election of that officer devolves upon the Senate. A.

Const., 12th amendment.

MEETING of Congress. The Congress shall assemble at least once in every year, and such meeting shall be on the first Monday in December, unless they shall by law appoint a different day.

Const., art. 1., sec. 4, cl. 2.

MEMBERS of the Senate.—(See *Senators.*)

Names of the members. The yeas and nays of the members of either house, on any question, shall, at the desire of one-fifth of those present, be entered on the journal, &c.

Const., art. 1, sec. 5, cl. 3.

NOMINATE. The President shall nominate, and, by and with the advice and consent of the Senate, shall appoint ambassadors, other public ministers, and consuls, judges of the Supreme Court, and all other officers of the United States whose appointments are not herein otherwise provided for, and which shall be established by law.

Const., art. 2, sec. 2, cl. 2.

Oath of office of senators and President of the Senate under 6th article of the Constitution : "I, A. B., do solemnly swear (or affirm, as the case may be) that I will support the Constitution of the United States." "The President of the Senate, for the time being, shall also administer the said oath or affirmation to each senator who shall hereafter be elected previous to his taking his seat And in any future case of a President of the Senate, who shall not have taken the said oath or affirmation, the same shall be administered to him by any one of the members of the Senate."—(See act of Congress, approved June 1, 1789.)

OATH of the Secretary of the Senate under the 6th article of the Constitution and the act of June 1, 1789 : "I, A. B., do solemnly swear (or affirm, as the case may be) that I will support the Constitution of the United States."

OATH of office of the Secretary of the Senate, under the act of Congress of June 1, 1789 : "I, A. B., Secretary of the Senate of the United States of America, do solemnly swear, or affirm, that I will truly and faithfully discharge the duties of my said office, to the best of my knowledge and abilities."

OFFICE. No senator or representative shall, during the time for which he was elected, be appointed to any civil office under the authority of the United States which shall have been created or the emoluments whereof shall have been increased during such time.

Const., art. 1, sec. 6, cl. 9.

OFFICERS. The Senate shall choose their own officers, and also a President *pro tempore*, in the absence of the Vice-President.

Const., art. 1, sec. 3, cl. 5.

ORDER, resolution, or vote, to which the concurrence of the Senate and House of Representatives may be necessary, except on questions of adjournment, shall be presented to the President, &c.

Const., art. 1, sec. 7, cl. 3.

ORIGINATE. All bills for raising revenue shall originate in the House of Representatives.

Const., art. 1, sec. 7, cl. 1.

ORIGINATED Every bill, resolution, order, or vote not approved, shall be returned by the President, with his objections, to that house in which it shall have originated.

Const., art. 1, sec. 7, cl. 2.

Penalties. Each house may be authorized to compel the attendance of absent members in such manner and under such penalties as each house may provide.

Const., art. 1, sec. 5, cl. 1.

POWER. The Senate shall have the sole power to try all impeachments.

Const., art. 1, sec. 3, cl. 6.

POWERS herein granted vested in Congress. All legislative.

Const., art. 1, sec. 1, cl. 1.

PRESENTED. Every bill, order, resolution, or vote to which the concurrence of the Senate and House of Representatives may be necessary, &c., shall be presented to the President.

Const., art. 1, sec. 7, cl. 2, 3.

PRESIDENT of the Senate. The Vice-President of the United States shall be President of the Senate, but shall have no vote unless they be equally divided.

Const., art. 1, sec. 3, cl. 4.

PRESIDENT *pro tempore*. The Senate shall choose their other officers and also a President *pro tempore*, in the absence of the Vice-President, or when he shall exercise the office of President of the United States.

Const., art. 1, sec. 3, cl. 5.

PRESIDENT of the Senate. The lists of votes of electors of President and Vice-President shall be directed to the President of the Senate.

Const., 12th amendment.

PRESIDENT of the Senate The President of the Senate shall, in the presence of the Senate and House of Representatives, open all the certificates of the electors of President and Vice-President of the United States.

Const., 12th amendment.

PRESIDENT of the United States. The Senate shall choose a President *pro tempore* when the Vice-President shall act as President of the United States.

Const., art. 1, sec. 3, cl. 5.

PRESIDENT of the United States is tried by the Senate on an impeachment the Chief Justice shall preside. When the.

Const., art. 1, sec. 3, cl. 6.

PRESIDENT of the United States.   Every bill which shall have passed the House of Representatives and Senate shall be presented to the President; if he approve, he shall sign it; but if not, he shall return it, with his objections, to that house in which it shall have originated, &c.

Const., art. 1, sec. 7, cl. 2.

PRESIDENT of the United States.   If any bill shall not be returned by the President within ten days (Sundays excepted) after it shall have been presented to him, the same shall be a law, in like manner as if he had signed it, unless the Congress, by their adjournment, prevent its return, in which case it shall not be a law, &c.

Const., art. 1, sec. 7, cl. 2.

PRESIDENT of the United States   Every order, resolution, or vote to which the concurrence of the Senate and House of Representatives may be necessary (except on a question of adjournment) shall be presented to the President of the United States, and, before the same shall take effect, shall be approved by him, or, being disapproved by him, shall be repassed by two-thirds of the Senate and House of Representatives.

Const., art. 1, sec. 7, cl. 3.

PRESIDENT of the United States.   He shall have power, by and with the advice and consent of the Senate, to make treaties, provided two-thirds of the senators present concur; and he shall nominate, and, by and with the advice and consent of the Senate, shall appoint ambassadors, other public ministers, and consuls, judges of the Supreme Court, and all other officers of the United States whose appointments are not herein otherwise provided for, and which shall be established by law; but the Congress may by law vest the appointment of such inferior officers as they think proper in the President alone, in the courts of law, or in the heads of departments.

Const., art. 2, sec. 2, cl. 2.

PRESIDENT of the United States.   The President shall have power to fill up all vacancies that may happen during the recess of the Senate by granting commissions, which shall expire at the end of their next session.

Const., art. 2, sec. 2, cl. 3.

PRESIDENT of the United States.   He shall, from time to time, give to the Congress information of the state of the Union, and recommend to their consideration such measures as he shall judge necessary and expedient; he may, on extraordinary occasions, convene both houses, or either of them, and, in case of disagreement between them with respect to the time of adjournment, he may adjourn them to such time as he shall think proper; he shall receive ambassadors and other public ministers; he shall take care that the laws be faithfully executed, and shall commission all the officers of the United States.

Const., art. 2, sec. 3, cl. 1.

PRIVILEGED. Senators and representatives shall, in all cases, except treason, felony, and breach of the peace, he privileged from arrest during their attendance at the session of their respective houses, and in going to and returning from the same.

Const., art. 1, sec. 6, cl. 1.

PROCEEDINGS. Each house may determine the rules of its proceedings.

Const., art. 1, sec. 5. cl. 1.

PROCEEDINGS. Each house shall keep a journal of its proceedings.

Const., art. 1, sec. 5, cl. 3.

PUNISH. Each house of Congress may punish its members for disorderly behavior.

Const., art. 1, sec. 5, cl. 2.

Qualification of a senator in Congress shall be thirty years of age; nine years a citizen of the United States, and when elected an inhabitant of same State.

Const., art. 1, sec. 3, cl. 3.

QUALIFICATION to office. The senators shall be bound by oath or affirmation to support the Constitution of the United States.

Const., art. 6, sec. —, cl. 3.

QUALIFICATION of its own members. Each house of Congress shall be the judge of the elections, returns, and qualifications of its own members.

Const., art. 1, sec. 5, cl. 1.

QUALIFICATIONS of Vice-President the same as for President of the United States.

Const., 12th amendment.

QUESTION. The yeas and nays of the members of either house on any question shall, at the desire of one-fifth of those present, be entered on the journal.

Const., art. 1, sec. 5, cl. 3.

QUESTION. On question of adjournment of the two houses, the approbation of the President is not necessary.

Const., art. 1, sec. 7, cl. 3.

QUESTIONED. For any speech or debate in either house, they shall not be questioned in any other place.

Const., art. 1, sec. 6, cl. 1.

QUORUM. A majority of each house shall constitute a quorum to do business, but a smaller number may adjourn from day to day, and may be authorized to compel the attendance of absent members, in such manner, and under such penalties, as each house may provide.

Const., art. 1, sec. 5, cl. 1.

QUORUM of the Senate. A quorum (for the election of Vice-President by the Senate) shall consist of two-thirds of the whole number of senators, and a majority of the whole number shall be necessary to a choice.

Const., 12th amendment.

Recess of the Senate. The President shall have power to fill up all vacancies that may happen during the recess of the Senate, by granting commissions, which shall expire at the end of their next session.

Const., art. 2, sec. 2, cl. 3.

RECONSIDERED. Bills returned, with objections, by the President of the United States, to be reconsidered by the two houses, and if approved by two-thirds of both houses shall become a law.

Const., art. 1, sec. 7, cl. 2.

RECONSIDERED. Any order, resolution, or vote, returned with objections by the President, may be reconsidered and repassed by two-thirds of both houses.

Const., art. 1, sec. 7, cl. 3.

RESIGNATION. Vacancies, by resignation of senators, may be filled by the executive of a State in recess of legislature.

Const , art. 1, sec. 3, cl. 2.

RESOLUTION. Every order, resolution, or vote, to which the concurrence of the Senate and House of Representatives may be necessary, (except on a question of adjournment,) shall be presented to the President of the United States, and, before the same shall take effect, shall be approved by him ; or, being disapproved by him, shall be repassed by two-thirds of the Senate and House of Representatives, according to the rules and limitations prescribed in the case of a bill.—(See *Bills.*)

Const., art. 1, sec. 7, cl. 3.

RETURNED. Bills, resolutions, &c., not approved, to be returned by the President to the house in which they originated.

Const., art. 1, sec. 7, cl. 2.

RETURNED. Bills, resolutions, &c., not returned within ten days, Sundays excepted, to become laws, unless Congress adjourn.

Const., art. 1, sec. 7, cl. 2.

RETURNS. Each house shall be the judge of the elections, returns, and qualifications of its own members.

Const., art. 1, sec. 5, cl. 1.

REVENUE. All bills for raising revenue shall originate in the House of Representatives ; but the Senate may propose, or concur, with amendments, as on other bills.

Const., art. 1, sec. 7, cl. 1.

RULES of proceedings. Each house of Congress may determine the rules of its proceedings.

Const., art. 1, sec. 5, cl. 2.

Seat of government. Neither house, during the session of Congress, shall, without the consent of the other, adjourn for more than three days, nor to any other place than that in which the two houses shall be sitting.

Const., art. 1, sec. 5, cl. 4.

SEATS of senators.   Terms at which the seats of the several classes of senator shall be vacated.

Const., art. 1, sec. 3, cl. 2.

SECRECY.   Each house of Congress shall keep a journal of its proceedings, and, from time to time, publish the same, excepting such parts as may, in their judgment, require secrecy.

Const., art. 1, sec. 5, cl. 3.

SENATE and House of Representatives   The Congress of the United States shall consist of a Senate and House of Representatives.

Const., art. 1, sec. 1.

SENATE.   The Senate shall be composed of two senators from each State, chosen by the legislature for six years, and each senator shall have one vote.

Const., art. 1, sec. 3, cl. 1.

SENATE.   The Vice-President of the United States shall be President of the Senate, but shall have no vote unless they be equally divided.

Const., art. 1, sec. 3, cl. 4.

SENATE.   The Senate shall choose their other officers, and also a President *pro tempore* in the absence of the Vice-President, or when he shall exercise the office of President of the United States.

Const., art. 1, sec. 3, cl. 5.

SENATE.   The Senate shall have the sole power to try all impeachments; when sitting for that purpose they shall be on oath or affirmation.   When the President of the United States is tried the Chief Justice shall preside; and no person shall be convicted without the concurrence of two-thirds of the members present.

Const., art. 1, sec. 3, cl. 6.

SENATE.   The judgment of the Senate, in cases of impeachment, shall not extend further than to removal from office, and disqualification to hold and enjoy an office of honor, trust, or profit, under the United States; but the party convicted shall, nevertheless, be liable and subject to indictment, trial, judgment, and punishment according to law.

Const., art. 1, sec. 3, cl. 7.

SENATE.   The Senate shall be the judge of the elections, returns, and qualifications of its own members; a majority shall constitute a quorum to do business, but a smaller number may adjourn from day to day, and may be authorized to compel the attendance of absent members, in such manner, and under such penalties as each house may provide.

Const., art. 1, sec. 5, cl. 1.

SENATE.   The Senate may determine the rules of its proceedings, punish its members for disorderly behavior, and, with the concurrence of two-thirds, expel a member.

Const., art. 1, sec. 5, cl. 2.

SENATE. The Senate shall keep a journal of its proceedings, and from time to time publish the same, excepting such parts as may, in their judgment, require secrecy; and the yeas and nays of the members on any question shall, at the desire of one-fifth of those present, be entered on the journal.

Const., art. 1, sec. 5, cl. 3.

SENATE. The Senate shall not, during the session of Congress, without the consent of the House of Representatives, adjourn for more than three days, nor to any other place than that in which the two houses shall be sitting.

Const., art. 1, sec. 5, cl. 4.

SENATE. All bills for raising revenue shall originate in the House of Representatives, but the Senate may propose or concur with amendments, as on other bills. — (See *Bills.*)

Const., art. 1, sec. 7, cl. 1.

SENATE. Every bill, order, resolution, and vote, (except on a question of adjournment,) originating in either house of Congress, shall be presented to the President of the United States.

SENATE. President of Senate on bills, resolutions, orders, and votes.   (See *Bills.*)

SENATE   The President shall have power, by and with the advice and consent of the Senate, to make treaties, provided two-thirds of the senators present concur; and he shall nominate, and, by and with the advice and consent of the Senate, shall appoint ambassadors, other public ministers, and consuls, judges of the Supreme Court, and all other officers of the United States whose appointments are not herein otherwise provided for, and which shall be established by law. But the Congress may, by law, vest the appointment of such inferior officers as they shall think proper in the President alone, in the courts of law, or in the heads of departments.

Const., art. 2, sec. 2, cl. 2.

SENATE. The President shall have power to fill up all vacancies that may happen during the recess of the Senate, by granting commissions, which shall expire at the end of their next session.

Const., art. 2, sec. 2, cl. 3.

SENATE   The President may, on extraordinary occasions, convene both houses of Congress, or either of them.

Const., art. 2, sec. 3, cl. 1.

SENATE. No State, without its consent, shall be deprived of its equal suffrage in the Senate.

Const., art. 5.

SENATE. The lists of votes of electors of President and Vice-President shall be directed to the President of the Senate.

Const , 12th amendment.

SENATE. The President of the Senate shall, in presence of the Senate and House of Representatives, open all the certificates of the electors of President and Vice-President of the United States.

Const., 12th amendment.

SENATE. If no person have a majority of the electoral votes as Vice-President, then from the two highest numbers on the list the Senate shall choose the Vice-President; a quorum for the purpose shall consist of two-thirds of the whole number of senators, and a majority of the whole number shall be necessary to a choice.

Const., 12th amendment.

SENATOR. Each senator shall have one vote.

Const., art. 1, sec. 3, cl. 1.

SENATOR. No person shall be a senator who shall not have attained the age of thirty years, been nine years a citizen of the United States, and, when elected, an inhabitant of the State for which he shall be chosen.

Const., art. 1, sec. 3, cl. 3.

SENATOR. No senator or representative shall, during the time for which he was elected, be appointed to any civil office, under the authority of the United States, which shall have been created, or the emoluments whereof shall have been increased during such time; and no person holding any office under the United States shall be a member of either house during his continuance in office.

Const., art. 1, sec. 6, cl. 2.

SENATOR. No senator shall be appointed an elector of President or Vice-President of the United States.

Const., art. 2, sec. 1, cl. 2.

SENATORS. The Senate of the United States shall be composed of two senators from each State.

Const., art. 1, sec. 3, cl. 1.

SENATORS. Two senators shall be chosen by the legislature of each State for six years.

Const., art. 1, sec. 3, cl. 1.

SENATORS shall be divided as equally as may be into three classes. The seats of the senators of the first class shall be vacated at the expiration of the second year, of the second class at the expiration of the fourth year, and of the third class at the expiration of the sixth year, so that one-third may be chosen every second year; and if vacancies happen by resignation or otherwise during the recess of the legislature of any State, the executive thereof may make temporary appointments until the next meeting of the legislature, which shall then fill such vacancies.

Const., art. 1, sec. 3, cl. 2.

8

SENATORS. The times, places, and manner of holding elections for senators and representatives shall be prescribed in each state by the legislature thereof; but the Congress may at any time, by law, make or alter such regulations, except as to the places of choosing senators.

Const., art. 1, sec. 4, cl. 1.

SENATORS and representatives shall receive a compensation for their services, to be ascertained by law, and paid out of the treasury of the United States. They shall, in all cases except treason, felony, and breach of the peace, be privileged from arrest during their attendance at the session of their respective houses, and in going to and returning from the same; and for any speech or debate in either house they shall not be questioned in any other place.

Const., art. 1, sec. 6, cl. 1.

SENATORS of the United States shall be bound, by oath or affirmation, to support the Constitution of the United States.

Const., art. 6, ——, cl. 3.

SESSION. The Congress shall assemble at least once in every year, and such meeting or session shall be on the first Monday in December, unless they shall, by law, appoint a different day.

Const., art. 1, sec. 4, cl. 2.

SESSION. Neither house, during the session of Congress, shall, without the consent of the other, adjourn for more than three days, nor to any other place than that in which the two houses shall be sitting.

Const., art. 1, sec. 5, cl. 4.

SESSION. Senators and representatives shall, in all cases except treason, felony, and breach of the peace, be privileged from arrest during their attendance at the session of their respective houses, and in going to and returning from the same.

Const., art. 1, sec. 6, cl. 1.

SESSION. The President shall have power to fill up all vacancies that may happen during the recess of the Senate, by granting commissions which shall expire at the end of their next session.

Const., art. 2, sec. 2, cl. 3.

SIGNED. Every bill, resolution, order, or vote, approved, shall be signed by the President; and any bill, &c., not returned within ten days, (Sundays excepted, &c.,) shall become a law as if it had been signed by the President.

Const., art. 1, sec. 7, cl. 2.

SPEECH. Senators and representatives, for any speech or debate in either house, shall not be questioned in any other place.

Const., art. 1, sec. 6, cl. 1.

STATE The Senate of the United States shall be composed of two senators from each State, chosen by the legislature thereof.

Const., art. 1, sec. 3, cl. 1.

STATE. If vacancies happen in seats of senators, by resignation or otherwise, during the recess of the legislature of any State, the executive shall then fill such vacancies

Const., art. 1, sec. 3, cl. 2.

STATE. A senator in Congress shall be an inhabitant of the State for which he shall be chosen.

Const., art. 1, sec. 3, cl. 3.

STATE. The times, places, and manner of holding elections for senators and representatives shall be prescribed in each State by the legislature thereof; but the Congress may at any time, by law, make or alter such regulations, except as to the places of choosing senators.

Const., art. 1, sec. 4, cl. 1.

STATE. No State, without its consent, shall be deprived of its equal suffrage in the Senate.

Const., art. 5.

SUFFRAGE. No State, without its consent, shall be deprived of its equal suffrage in the Senate.

Const., art. 5.

SUNDAYS excepted. Ten days allowed the President to return a bill, resolution, &c., Sundays excepted.

Const., art. 1, sec. 7, cl. 2.

SUPPORT the Constitution. The senators, representatives, &c., shall be bound by an oath to support the Constitution.

Const., art. 6, sec. 1, cl. 3.

Term of office of senators in Congress; to be chosen for six years.

Const., art. 1, sec. 3, cl. 1.

TERM of citizenship, as qualification for a senator in Congress, nine years.

Const., art. 1, sec. 3, cl. 3.

TREASON. For treason a senator or representative may be arrested.

Const., art. 1, sec. 6, cl. 1.

TREASURY. The senators and representatives shall receive a compensation for their services, to be ascertained by law, and paid out of the treasury of the United States.

Const., art 1, sec. 6, cl. 1.

TREATIES. The President shall have power, by and with the advice and consent of the Senate, to make treaties, provided two-thirds of the senators present concur.

Const., art. 2, sec. 2, cl. 2.

64 PROVISIONS IN THE CONSTITUTION

Two-THIRDS. No person shall be convicted by the Senate on an impeachment without the concurrence of two-thirds of the members present.

Const., art. 1, sec. 3, cl. 6.

Two-THIRDS. Each house of Congress may, by the concurrence of two-thirds, expel a member.

Const., art. 1, sec. 5, cl. 2.

Two-THIRDS. Bills returned with objections by the President may be passed by two-thirds of both houses of Congress and become a law.

Const., art. 1, sec. 7, cl. 2.

Two-THIRDS. Any order, resolution, or vote to which the concurrence of the Senate and House of Representatives may be necessary, (except on a question of adjournment,) and returned with objections by the President, may be repassed by two-thirds of both houses of Congress.

Const., art. 1, sec. 7, cl. 8.

Two-THIRDS. The President shall have power, by and with the advice and consent of the Senate, to make all treaties, provided two-thirds of the senators present concur.

Const., art. 2, sec. 3, cl. 2.

Two-THIRDS. The Congress, whenever two-thirds of both houses shall deem it necessary, shall propose amendments to this Constitution.

Const., art. 5.

Two-THIRDS A quorum (for the election of Vice-President by the Senate) shall consist of two-thirds of the whole number of senators, and a majority of the whole number shall be necessary to a choice.

Const., 12th amendment.

Vacancies happen, by resignation or otherwise, in the seats of senators during the recess of the legislature of any State, the executive thereof may make temporary appointments until the next meeting of the legislature, which shall then fill such vacancies. If.

Const., art. 1, sec. 3, cl. 2.

VACANCIES. The President shall have power to fill up all vacancies that may happen during the recess of the Senate by granting commissions, which shall expire at the end of their next session.

Const., art. 2, sec. 2, cl. 3.

VESTED in a Congress. All legislative powers herein granted shall be vested in a Congress of the United States, which shall consist of a Senate and House of Representatives.

Const., art. 1, sec. 1, cl. 1.

VICE-President shall have no vote in the Senate unless they be equally divided. The.

Const., art. 1, sec. 3, cl. 4.

Vice-President, or when he shall exercise the office of President of the United States. The Senate shall choose a President *pro tempore* in the absence of the.

Const., art. 1, sec. 3, cl. 5

Vice-President. The President shall hold his office during the term of four years, and, together with the Vice-President, chosen for the same term, be elected as follows, &c.

Const., 12th amendment.

Vice-President of the United States. Qualification required as Vice-President same as for President of the United States.

Const., 12th amendment.

Vice-President. In case of the removal of the President from office, or of his death, resignation, or inability to discharge the powers and duties of the said office, the same shall devolve on the Vice-President, and the Congress may by law provide for the case of removal, death, resignation, or inability, both of the President and Vice-President, declaring what officer shall then act as President, and such officer shall act accordingly until the disability be removed or a President shall be elected.

Const., art. 2, sec. 1, cl. 5.

Vice-President shall be removed from office on impeachment for and conviction of treason, bribery, or other high crimes and misdemeanors. The.

Const., art. 2, sec. 4, cl. 1.

Vice-President. Election of Vice-President of the United States.

Const., 12th amendment.

Vice-President. The lists of votes of electors of President and Vice-President shall be directed to the President of the Senate.

Const., 12th amendment.

Vice-President. The President of the Senate shall, in presence of the Senate and House of Representatives, open all the certificates of the electors of President and Vice-President of the United States.

Const., 12th amendment.

Vice-President. If the House of Representatives shall not choose a President, whenever the right of choice shall devolve upon them, before the 4th day of March next following, then the Vice-President shall act as President, as in the case of the death or other constitutional disability of the President.

Const., 12th amendment.

Vice-President. The person having the greatest number of votes as Vice-President shall be the Vice-President, if such number be a majority of the whole number of electors appointed ; and if no person have a majority, then, from the two highest numbers on the list, the Senate shall choose the Vice-President : a quorum for the purpose shall consist of two-thirds of the whole number of senators, and a majority of the whole number shall be necessary to a choice. But no person constitutionally ineligible to the office of President shall be eligible to that of Vice-President of the United States.

Const., 12th amendment.

VOTE. Each senator shall have one vote.

Const., art. 1, sec. 3, cl. 1.

VOTE. The Vice-President shall have no vote unless the Senate be equally divided.

Const., art. 1, sec. 3, cl. 4.

VOTE. Every vote to which the concurrence of the Senate and House of Representatives may be necessary (except on a question of adjournment) shall be presented to the President.

Const., art. 1, sec. 7, cl. 3.

VOTES in the two houses of Congress on passage of any bill, order, resolution, or vote, returned with objections by the President, shall be taken by yeas and nays.

Const., art. 1, sec. 7, cl. 2, 3.

VOTES of electors of President and Vice-President. The place and manner of giving the votes; lists of votes to be made, signed, certified, transmitted sealed to the seat of government, directed to the President of the Senate, to be opened and counted by that officer in the presence of the Senate and House of Representatives; the number necessary to a choice; the day on which electoral votes shall be given throughout the United States.

Const., 12th amendment.

Yeas and nays of the members of either house of Congress, on any question, shall, at the desire of one-fifth of those present, be entered on the journal. The.

Const., art. 1, sec. 5, cl. 3.

YEAS and nays. Votes in the two houses of Congress on passage of any bill, order, resolution, or vote, returned with objections by the President, shall be taken by yeas and nays.

Const., art. 1, sec. 7, cl. 2, 3.